THE END
OF AN ALLIANCE

Rome's Defection from the Axis in 1943

FRIEDRICH-KARL von PLEHWE

With a Foreword by F. W. D. Deakin

Translated from the German by Eric Mosbacher

LONDON
OXFORD UNIVERSITY PRESS
NEW YORK TORONTO
1971

Oxford University Press, Ely House, London W.1

GLASGOW   NEW YORK   TORONTO   MELBOURNE   WELLINGTON
CAPE TOWN   SALISBURY   IBADAN   NAIROBI   DAR ES SALAAM   LUSAKA   ADDIS ABABA
BOMBAY   CALCUTTA   MADRAS   KARACHI   LAHORE   DACCA
KUALA LUMPUR   SINGAPORE   HONG KONG   TOKYO

ISBN 0 19 215938 0

© 1967 by Verlag Ullstein GmbH, Frankfurt/M.—Berlin

Printed in Great Britain by
Richard Clay (The Chaucer Press) Ltd
Bungay, Suffolk

Foreword

THIS book deals with one of the most dramatic events of the Second World War —the breakdown of the Axis pact of 1939 between Germany and Italy, under the gathering shadows of military defeat. It describes, in a spirit of objective inquiry, based on special inside knowledge and personal experience, the last stages of the alliance leading to its breakdown and the seeking by the Badoglio government of an armistice with the Western Allies in early September 1943.

The author has presented his account in model fashion. He has, with deliberation, based his narrative, which is enriched by fresh and imaginative reflections on the confusion of the Roman scene, on an analysis of Italian–German relations as seen at the time and constructed within his own experience.

Drawing on notes and personal records made at the time, the author has distilled his personal impressions and knowledge of events as a model of history 'as it really was', refraining from facile judgements of hindsight and drawing sparingly on subsequent documentation and olympian pronouncements of historians only to illustrate a passing detail. It seems that such a combination has a special value and attraction for delivering contributions to historical research.

By the summer of 1943 the Allies had cleared the Axis forces from North Africa and landed in Sicily. The invasion of Continental Italy loomed; the threat to the fortress of the Reich beyond the frontiers of the Alps would become a reality. The immediate shift of emphasis of the war, with the strategic initiative now firmly in Anglo-American hands, was drawn to the Mediterranean.

The Germans were on the defensive on the Eastern front, their main reserves and resources stretched to the limit, and needed in this theatre to hold a major Russian assault.

In the Southern theatre, the Italian ally was facing a crisis in which political and military elements were inextricably mixed. The issue was deceptive in its simplicity. Could the Axis meet an Anglo-American invasion in military terms and under what conditions? Would the Fascist régime of Mussolini survive internal disorder and a possible *coup d'état* in event of an Allied landing?

The German High Command had no real choice. Italy could be defended by massive reinforcements of élite divisions and war material, but only at the expense of risking major disaster on the Russian front, and uncovering the Western defences constructed against an Anglo-American landing in northern France inevitable and inscrutable in its timing.

Italy could survive as military ally only if German military aid on a massive scale were forthcoming. The alternative would be—and Mussolini had pressed Hitler since the winter of 1942—either a separate peace with Russia, or armistice negotiations with the Western Allies and the transition of Italy's position to that of a neutral in the final stages of the conflict.

The German military representatives in Rome, including the author, had no illusions as to the risk of a Fascist collapse. The Ambassador, Hans-Georg von Mackensen, in his 'lonely' reports—the manner of their composition is vividly described by the author—presented to Berlin the 'official' views of the Rome government. He had no contact with the incipient treason of certain Fascist leaders nor the shadowing considerations of a political alternative emerging under the protection of the Court. No hint of imminent political disintegration escapes from his dispatches.

The contacts of General von Rintelen and the author with the Italian Supreme Command and their Chiefs of Staff were very close. There was an instinctive bond of genuine loyalty between the two allied officer corps. The author had been attached before the war to the Turin Military Academy, and early friendships made there proved invaluable to him in his present post, not clouding his judgement, but bringing him accurate intelligence, and creating proven loyalties.

In general terms, the German military mission and Marshal Kesselring (of whom Dr. von Plehwe presents a fair portrait) based all their assumptions on the premise that the Italian army would be able to continue to fight only if decisively reinforced by Germany.

The story of the total frustration of this mission led by Rintelen forms the essence of this book. It was also in the nature of things that Hitler would never accept the disappearance of Mussolini as a political and ideological partner.

All parties, German and Italian, were taken by surprise, as the author describes in cool and vivid terms, by the *coup d'état* which ousted Mussolini on 26 July 1943, but the assessment of its consequences on the German side, as revealed in detail for the first time in this book with quiet authority and fresh insight, involved an exacerbation of personal conflicts and loyalties in the minds of the mentors of the German Embassy and military personalities stationed in Rome.

As some of the Italian officers in touch with their German colleagues, and even the reserved character of General Ambrosio, the Chief of the Italian Staff, adroitly hinted to them, perhaps the only ultimate solution for them all would be a similar military *coup* in Germany to be followed by genuine collaboration between the German and Italian military commands to fight a series of delaying actions against the Allies with a view to a joint approach to an ultimate peace settlement.

But the thought that the example of Rome could be followed in Berlin invited desperate and fearful speculation. The brutal vendetta against the King of Italy and Marshal Badoglio as the successor to Mussolini at the head of affairs which Hitler conceived in the hours following the latter's fall and disappearance produced a discouraging and sinister answer to any such illusions.

Hitler's plan to seize the King and Badoglio together with members of his administration by a commando operation and to restore Mussolini and Italian Fascism was not supported but resisted on the spot by the leading German military representatives in Rome. The details of this episode are clarified for the first time in this account with a wealth of new detail. A temporary breathing

space was precariously gained, and in particular by the courageous personal intervention of Rintelen himself at Hitler's headquarters.

The German High Command had long considered the direct military occupation of Italy north of the Apenines, and plans existed for such a move. There was much talk of treason in both camps, Italian and German, and the meetings in August between military representatives on both sides, and the journey of Ribbentrop to Tarvisio at the beginning of the month heightened the atmosphere of mutual distrust. But as Jodl put it after the final débâcle, 'We had to avoid doing anything to give the Italians a moral excuse for their treachery or by premature hostile action actually to commit treachery ourselves'.

The Tarvisio meeting on 8 August proved to be the last chance of continued Italian–German military co-operation.

The author is convinced that up to this point the fragile combination held together and that the majority of the Italian officer corps itself 'could conceive of the final stage of the war only in agreement with Germany'. Badoglio wanted to find out whether there was a slight hope that he could come to terms with the Germans in collaboration, to seek a joint end to the war.

The subsequent attempts of his Italian apologists to show that from the moment of his assumption of office he intended to seek a secret agreement with the Western Allies is not proved, and represents an apologetic antedating.

On the issue of 'treason' and the unilateral breach of treaty obligations, Dr. von Plehwe is convinced, on deep reflection, that by the summer of 1943 any such formal commitments had lapsed, nor does he hold, as has been aired by some later writers, that in the final armistice negotiations the Badoglio emissaries were offering the Allies the German divisions in Italy as a 'dowry'.

The responsibility for the decision to withdraw from the war inherited from Mussolini himself by Badoglio, with the backing of the King, is studied here with the sympathy of intimate personal experience, and with the objectivity of a trained reporter of events. His account is all the more poignant in its illustration of the dilemma of one German official serving a régime for which he has a fearful antipathy, and as showing how the 'vantage-point of Rome' had become by 1943 an anxious and key listening post for similar precursory signs of the inescapable dilemma of Berlin.

Dr. von Plehwe admits the significance to himself, and to those who felt like him, of his emotional solidarity with his Italian military colleagues—hence perhaps a touch of excessive and real anxiety to go to the limits of justifying every action of Badoglio, Ambrosio, and the Italian leaders—and also how this led to a brief probing on the edge of the July Plot by himself and certain of his colleagues in Rome. (A visit from Gisevius at this time provides a revealing episode.)

Hitler's desire for revenge after the fall of Mussolini and for 'a modern St. Bartholomew's Night' in Rome was a savage pointer to a common fate, which might engulf both worlds.

As the author puts it with dignity, 'I was young, still just thirty-one, the product of a Prussian family and a strict classical schooling . . . I was thus totally unprepared to grapple with a situation in which there had been a complete reversal of values by the present rulers of Germany. My dislike of them had

steadily increased and long since turned into loathing. On that 31 July (the day of the planned commando operation of General Student) it was tempting to draw the last bitter consequence, that is, to join my Italian friends if it came to a final breach. I had in fact already discussed this possibility at home.'

Such a question was real during these critical days. By a narrow margin the German military mission was able to remain at its post and gain time until the inevitable break in the alliance in early September 1943 ended their work.

This book is not an apologia but a record, which stands the test of historical investigation, of the striving of the German military representatives in Rome to smooth the hardships of the situation and to avoid any superfluous sacrifices in those crucial weeks of increasing embitterment between the Germans and the Italian leadership.

F. W. D. Deakin

Contents

Foreword by F. W. D. Deakin   iii

Key to abbreviations in footnotes   ix

Preface   xi

  I   Crisis of the Alliance   1

  II   Dictator's Downfall   39

 III   The Alliance Falls Apart   107

Index   153

Key to Abbreviations in Footnotes

A.A. Pol. Arch. Politisches Archiv des Auswärtigen Amts bis 1945, Büro Staatsekretär und Büro Reichsminister.

MGFA DZ Militärgeschichtliches Forschungsamt, Dokumentzentrale, Freiburg in Breisgau.

ADAP, D *Akten zur deutschen auswärtigen Politik 1918–1945*, Serie D, Bonn, 1964.

Ktb. OKW *Kriegstagebuch des Oberkommando der Wehrmacht*, ed. P. E. Schramm, Vol. III, Frankfurt, 1963.

Lage *Hitlers Lagebesprechungen*, ed. Helmut Heiber, Stuttgart, 1962.

Anfuso Filippo Anfuso, *Rom–Berlin im diplomatischen Spiel*, Essen, 1951.

Badoglio Pietro Badoglio, *Italien im Zweiten Weltkrieg*, Munich, undated.

Bonomi Ivanoe Bonomi, *Diario di un Anno*, Milan, 1953.

Castellano, Giuseppe Castellano, *Come firmai l'armistizio di Cassibile*, Milan,
L'armistizio 1945.

Castellano, Giuseppe Castellano, *La guerra continua*, Milan 1963.
La guerra

Deakin F. W. D. Deakin, *The Brutal Friendship*, London, 1962.

Goebbels *Goebbels Tagebücher*, ed. Louis P. Lochner, Zürich, 1948.

Grandi *Dino Grandi Racconta*, place of publication not stated, 1945.

Guariglia Raffaele Guariglia, *Ricordi 1922–1946*, Naples, 1950.

Kesselring Albert Kesselring, *Soldat bis zum letzten Tag*, Bonn, 1954.

Kirkpatrick Sir Ivone Kirkpatrick, *Mussolini*, London, 1964.

Puntoni Paolo Puntoni, *Parla Vittorio Emanuele III*, Milan, 1958.

Rintelen Enno von Rintelen, *Mussolini als Bundesgenosse*, Tübingen and Stuttgart, 1951.

Warlimont Walter Warlimont, *Im Hauptquartier der deutschen Wehrmacht 1939–1945*, Frankfurt, 1962.

Wiskemann Elizabeth Wiskemann, *The Rome–Berlin Axis*, London, 1949.

Preface

THIS book was intended to be primarily an account of personal experience. The suggestion that I should write it was made as long ago as the immediate post-war period by a number of historians at Göttingen, including my respected teacher Professor S. A. Kaehler and Professors Hermann Aubin and Walter Bussmann.

The year 1943 was crowded with events the consequence of which led to the final collapse of the Third Reich and brought to an end the most disastrous period of German history. It began with the tragedy of Stalingrad, which was followed by the loss of the Axis position in North Africa and the break up of the German–Italian alliance. It is this last dramatic and ominous event that is to be described here.

From November 1940 to the autumn of 1943 I was on the staff of the Military Attaché at the German Embassy in Rome. The Ambassador was Hans-Georg von Mackensen, the eldest son of Field-Marshal August von Mackensen, and the Military Attaché was General Enno von Rintelen. Since 1940 the latter had also been responsible for the co-ordination of all questions arising from the conduct of the war in the Mediterranean area, and he had therefore been given the additional title of German General at Italian Army Headquarters. As a result of my appointment as First Staff Officer, (1a) of the Military Attaché in Rome and German General at Italian Army Headquarters I became involved in this double task. The appointment turned out to cover an extremely interesting, wide-ranging field of duties concerned with all the political and military problems of the alliance. They included securing smooth co-operation in German and Italian operations in all the southern theatres of war: Albania and Greece, Yugoslavia, Libya, and Egypt, the Dodecanese and the Aegean, Tunisia, and finally Sicily. They also included all basic problems involved in the use of Italian troops in Russia and Italian participation in the occupation of France.

In view of the always acute supply problem, the requirements of the war oversea were a source of continual concern. The Italians

were familiar with the problems of this kind of operation, of which the Germans had little experience. The consequence was continual differences of opinion.

Co-operation with an ally the size of Italy was itself a novelty in German history. Alliances had hitherto been generally against Germany. Germany took the step of entering an alliance of the type of the Rome–Berlin Axis with no experience worth mentioning of fighting a coalition war. The alliance with Austria in the First World War was no adequate precedent. Apart from other differences, the field of operations was incomparably smaller, and there were no language difficulties.

The unusual nature of the work of the top-level military–political liaison staff in Italy was the result of the number of fronts that had to be taken into account. Normally we should have had to concern ourselves only with the enemy's actions and intentions as well as those of the German and Italian commands, but in this case there was an additional complication.

In all negotiations with the Italians a distinction had to be made between Fascists and opponents of the régime. The progressive estrangement from Fascism was most evident in the Italian officers' corps. To us it was significant that far greater political and military insight was generally to be found among Italians who were critical of the Fascist system. They therefore deserved support. They also enjoyed our personal sympathy.

Finally, our greatest difficulties arose increasingly from our attitude to our own government. The insight into the mentality and intentions of Hitler and his entourage that this work in Rome gave us put us in a dilemma between duty and conscience, discipline and a rebellious sense of honour.

The chief sources for this account are the diaries that I kept at the time. These give precise dates and times of events, and also include numerous longer notes. These were written from time to time to provide a record of views of the situation as they existed at the time. In the autumn of 1943 the diaries and notes were put in a secure hiding-place, and with the help of trusted friends they were returned to my possession many years later, slightly nibbled by mice but still easily legible.

As they were used as the basis for a book not published till twenty-four years after the events described, a study of the literature on the subject that had been published in the meantime was

inevitable. The result was that an account of personal experience unintentionally developed into an attempt at an historical assessment, and for this, apart from my own records and the published literature, a firm foundation was provided by the documents of the old Foreign Ministry and the German High Command that were returned from the United States to Germany a few years ago. These were examined in the political archives of the Foreign Ministry in Bonn and the Military History Research Office at Freiburg.

All other sources are mentioned in the footnotes. Most of them are the accounts and memoirs that refer to the whole duration of the German–Italian alliance, and hence deal only summarily with portentous events of the summer of 1943. For a full account of the whole period Professor F. W. D. Deakin's massive and conscientious *The Brutal Friendship* (1962) was of the greatest assistance. But the events that form the substance of my story, that is, the violent German reactions to Mussolini's downfall and the resulting Italian predicament, are dealt with relatively cursorily by Deakin, who himself describes them as complicated and confused. There is therefore reason to hope that the survey that follows will contribute to filling a gap.

The Italian literature on the period is not easy to assess. In many cases the writer's purpose of defending his actions in retrospect stands out even more plainly than it does in German memoirs. Also accounts are often distorted by temperamental reciprocal accusations, and developments in Italy after 1943 followed paths even more tortuous than those in Germany after 1945. The Italian monarchy, after Fascism had been overthrown with its aid, first enjoyed high repute, but in 1946 a Republic was proclaimed and, consciously or unconsciously, the politicians and generals who wrote their memoirs tended to adapt themselves to this change in the history of their country. Hence we find instances in which they tone down the loyalty they showed to the dynasty in the course of 1943 and 1944. Also the memoirs and biographies often show a retrospective desire to antedate as far as possible their distaste for and opposition to the German–Italian alliance. This is especially striking in Vanna Vailati's two lives of Marshal Badoglio. In these the sequence of events is partly deliberately left out of account or an attempt is made by demonstrably incorrect dating to antedate decisive action on Badoglio's part.

So that my 1943 notes may serve the purpose of reflecting as faithfully as possible the situation as it seemed then, I include criticism of measures or individuals as it was made. In many cases the time that has since elapsed now enables events to be seen in a somewhat milder light. Also a better understanding of predicaments has resulted here and there in retrospective modification of more bristly views held in the heat of the moment.

As the material is based on diaries, use of the first person was unavoidable in many places.

In apportioning blame and responsibility for mistakes I expect to be criticized for dealing too leniently with the Italians and too severely with the Germans. It must, however, be borne in mind that in the summer of 1943 the German leadership, after suffering severe defeats on all fronts, was struggling desperately to maintain itself and resorted to brutal measures in the process. It thereby continually put itself objectively and morally in the wrong in relation to the Italians, who were trying to extricate themselves from a disastrous political and moral involvement. Nevertheless, in view of many things that happened before and during the Second World War, history certainly has no white toga in store for the Italians. Their copybook is sufficiently blotted by pre-war bellicosity of language, the irresponsible Abyssinian war of 1935, the senseless attack on Greece in the autumn of 1940, and the disgraceful show trial at Verona in 1944, to mention just a few especially dubious items, all of which would have their place in a complete and systematic account of the German–Italian alliance—also based on personal experience—that remains a wish for the future.

I

Crisis of the Alliance

Meeting at Klessheim

In the spring of 1943 a carefully prepared German–Italian meeting in the grand manner was held at Klessheim Castle, near Salzburg. Hitler and Mussolini, accompanied by a large civilian and military entourage, discussed the worrying war situation from 7–10 April.

Mussolini's special train left Rome at 2 p.m. on 6 April. A carriage was put at the disposal of Ambassador von Mackensen and his suite. General von Rintelen, who was still suffering from the effects of injuries received in an aircraft crash, had to remain behind in Rome, and Colonel-General Ambrosio, the Chief of the Comando Supremo, had therefore suggested that I should go in his place. The Comando Supremo, which will often be mentioned in the course of this work, corresponded to the Oberkommando der Wehrmacht, the German High Command. Ambassador von Mackensen was accompanied by his permanent adviser, SS Obersturmbannführer* Dr. Eugen Dollmann, who had been Himmler's representative in Rome for many years.

During the night the train had to be shunted to a siding in the Alps for eight hours, because Mussolini could not sleep while the train was in motion because of the poor state of his health.

Towards evening I was invited to join the Italian officers in Ambrosio's saloon carriage, where a long conversation took place. Ambrosio intervened only occasionally. Those present were General Gandin, Admiral Girosi, Colonels Montezemolo and Gallo, Lieutenant-Colonel Gianuzzi, and Captain Hausbrandt. What I was told amounted to a précis of Italian worries, with which I was very familiar, because they were continually and fully reported to the German authorities by General von Rintelen. The following picture resulted.

The German–Italian bridgehead that had been established in

*Rank in SS hierarchy corresponding to that of lieutenant-colonel.

Tunisia since 10 November 1942 would shortly be liquidated by the allies, though Hitler and the German High Command maintained the opposite. With that the African theatre of war, which had swallowed up the best contingents of the Italian army, would be irretrievably lost to the Axis. The protracted struggle in North Africa had also cost Italy practically the whole of her merchant fleet and, except for a few insignificant remnants, the small and medium units of her navy, which had been sunk in convoy work. Because of the oil shortage, the heavy naval units could be operational only for a few hours; and committing them to action would be disastrous in the absence of the small and medium units essential for their security and tactical use.

The Italian air force had hardly been operational since the outbreak of war, as their types of aircraft did not correspond with modern needs. The wings that had originally been available had been used up in subsequent operations.

After the fall of Tunisia, the allies must be expected to deploy their forces for the invasion of Italy. The completely inadequately armed and no longer motorized, let alone mechanized, remnants of the Italian army would be of little use for its defence. Only one division still had tanks of an obsolete type.

Only a few units were available for guarding and defending the long coastline of the islands of Sicily, Sardinia, and Corsica and the Italian mainland itself; these were the so-called coastal defence divisions, which in reality amounted to no more than a warning system. They lacked the necessary weapons and equipment, as well as trained officers and n.c.o.s.

Italy's supply position made it impossible to take better precautionary measures. All the fit men of military age whom in previous years it had been possible to put into uniform and arm had been immediately sent to replace casualties in the many theatres of war, Libya, Tunisia, Russia, and the Balkans. True, there were still many civilians of military age in Italy in 1943, but the state could provide them neither with uniforms nor rifles. Italy was one of the poorest countries in Europe in raw materials, and the war in Abyssinia, intervention in Spain, and now the world war had sucked her dry.

In comparison with all this it counted for relatively little that the Italian armaments industry was in many respects not sufficiently rationalized and worked too much for its own profit. In

private conversation the staff of the Comando Supremo admitted this with shame and indignation. But, even with greater effort and more stream-lined organization, it would have been impossible to cope with the strain of the new warfare of *matériel*. The circumstance that probably weighed most heavily in the spring of 1943, however, was the increasing apathy to which the Italian armed forces and the Italian people were succumbing. In a country that still preserved a good deal of the political realism of the *civis romanus*, even the cleverest propaganda tirades could not prevent people from forming their own opinions. Now that the prospects were hopeless, and above all in view of the threat of invasion that overhung the country, there could be no hope of a *levée en masse*.

If the German ally wished to change the course of events, it must, in the view of the Italian military leaders, shift the centre of gravity of the war to the Mediterranean area. It must send military and air formations to Italy in sufficient strength to leave the allies no prospect of a successful invasion. At the same time it must greatly increase deliveries of equipment and supplies for the Italian armed forces and for local coast defence. The needs of the German forces in Russia made these Italian wishes illusory in advance. Since the Stalingrad disaster of 31 January 1943, the initiative had passed to the enemy on the eastern front also.

The Italian officers said that it was now evident how justified had been the suggestion, made several times by Mussolini to Hitler since 1942, that he should come to terms with the Russians, because otherwise the bow would be hopelessly over-stretched. In the forthcoming conversations it would therefore again be necessary to discuss ways and means of alleviating the strain of fighting a war on many fronts. The Comando Supremo had submitted a detailed brief to Mussolini and had asked him to speak frankly to Hitler.

To make it clear that the German political and military leadership could be in no doubt about the mood and situation in Italy, verbatim extracts follow from a report by the Military Attaché in Rome of 12 March 1943, which was drafted by me. I was able to keep a copy made at the time. It may be found surprising that it was still possible in that year to submit really outspoken reports, with only a few modifying phrases dictated by caution. It certainly needed the courage and self-control of General von Rintelen, of whom F. W. Deakin, the Oxford historian whom we mentioned

B

above, writes:[1] 'The German Military Attaché in Rome, General Enno von Rintelen, was the main and most reliable and most perceptive source of information on Italian affairs. He had been in this post since 1936, and was by far the best observer of the Italian scene. His reports and dispatches form the most accurate picture of events as seen from Rome during these years.'

The report of 12 March 1943 stated in part:

Since the American landing in North Africa and the loss of Libya, military circles in Italy, and all civilians as well, regard the situation there as practically hopeless. This manifests itself in the military field in increased work on coastal defence which, however, is generally carried out only with lethargy, as the Italians regard the expected loss of the African theatre of war as a turning-point of quite special significance. They regard it as a sign of having been finally thrown back on the defensive.

In the field of morale, a mood of universal fatalism has set in. Even Italian officers emphasise in conversation that they think only from day to day, and in view of the situation in the Mediterranean no longer have an objective in view.

On the other hand, there are also circles that refuse to succumb to fatalism and would like to draw some sort of conclusion in order to save what still can be saved. The number and the resources of these individuals at the present time is not very great, and it will remain limited so long as the State system keeps political power in its hands and also above all so long as the Duce remains healthy and strong.

Every Italian knows that all strength and aid comes only from Germany. This is seen in particular by the veteran Fascists, who would be unable to retain their positions without a strong Germany and their country's dependence on it. The Italian officers' corps is bitter at the minor role that the Italian army plays in comparison with the German, as it was led into the war so irresponsibly badly prepared.

The last big speech by Reich Minister Dr. Goebbels attracted a great deal of attention in Italy. It was in part wrongly reported and/or wrongly understood here. It seems advisable to urge the Italian civilian information services to arrange for better and more accurate reporting in future.

Individual Italians (e.g., officers in the army and the militia) have since then felt obliged to express their concern about possible future domestic political developments in Germany. They added that nearly all Italians were very worried about this point, even though few dared mention it. They said that the Italian people, which was so firmly

[1] Deakin, p. 24.

rooted in religion, had an insuperable dislike, both emotionally and intellectually, of all radical socialist trends and methods smacking of Bolshevism. Hence it would be dismayed by any difference from their German ally that appeared in this field. There was also a lack of understanding of the treatment of the Jews on the German side and of German policy in relation to Catholicism, while in Italy the importance and influence of the Church was increasing as a direct consequence of the prolongation of the war. The Italian military leadership was actually making increased use of the Church (by increasing the number and enhancing the status of military chaplains, for instance), in order to improve the morale of Italian troops in accordance with the upbringing of the Italian people.

It is only this very deep-rooted attitude to life that has made it possible for individual Italians actually to say that it would be better for Italy for the British to come into the country before the possibility of further unfavourable developments of the war in the east brought Bolshevism to the gates of Italy.

A general cooling off in the attitude to German troops committed to the Mediterranean area is becoming noticeable in Italy. This is necessarily connected with the length of the war and of contact with them. There is also the fact that Italian officers and men were full of admiration and confidence in the always victorious strength of the Germany army, but now, because of setbacks in Russia and Africa, have grave doubts whether Germany can win the war by the force of arms.

Colonel von Buttlar, of the Army General Staff, confirmed a few days later that this report, like all the substantial or specially important reports of General von Rintelen, was immediately submitted to Hitler.

Such, in broad outline, was the situation in the Mediterranean area when the conversations at Klessheim began. The Italian alarm at the prospect of the early loss of Tunis, which they regarded as inevitable, must again be emphasized.

After the arrival at Klessheim on 7 April, a small but significant incident took place that remains indelibly in my memory. All the German and Italian personalities, State Secretaries, Gauleiters, generals and their suite, numbering about fifty or sixty altogether, waited in the big entrance hall of the castle while Hitler and Mussolini had a preliminary conversation with Ribbentrop and Under-Secretary of State Bastianini, the head of the Italian Foreign Ministry, in a neighbouring room. When the two heads of government emerged into the hall again and Hitler was about to accom-

pany his guest to the door, the buzz of conversation died down and all those present stood to attention facing the dictators. Hitler glanced to the right and noticed SS Obersturmbannführer Doll-mann standing in the background. He left Mussolini, made his way through the throng standing in front of Dollmann, and shook hands with him. I was standing so close that I could see the look of greeting in the eyes of the two accomplices. Hitler's lips moved briefly, but what he said was inaudible to those standing round. Then he again joined Mussolini, who had had to wait for a few moments. Hitler had so far greeted no one else among those present, not even his Italian guests. It was a striking confirmation of the status enjoyed by Dollmann, Himmler's envoy in Rome.

At Klessheim Dollman made the following remark to two German officers: 'As we see, the situation is deteriorating. Now you [by this he meant the Wehrmacht] will have to step up your efforts.'

Unfortunately the officers he addressed, one of whom was actually very much senior to him, failed to give the appropriate reply, which was that it was highly inappropriate to imply in this way that the tremendous efforts and sacrifices of the German troops had hitherto been insufficient.

We shall be referring to Dollmann again in connection with the events of 25 July 1943.

The negotiations at Klessheim were a great disappointment to the Italians. All political suggestions for improving the situation were rejected out of hand by Hitler, Göring, and Ribbentrop. There could be no question of coming to terms with Russia. Hitler's purpose in life was the total destruction of Communism by the force of arms, and he was certainly going to achieve it; and it was foolish in wartime to suggest entering into premature negotiations with the enemy. Such a course could at best be considered only after a great success.

The Italians, however, took the view that such success against the Russians could no longer be hoped for. Bastianini stoutly argued the necessity of announcing as a war aim a charter for the European countries under German and Italian occupation, offering them the prospect of a meaningful 'new order' in Europe, and hence making possible a minimum of confidence in Germany and Italy. Hitler and Ribbentrop declared this idea to be undiscussable. It would be interpreted merely as weakness.

Let us anticipate the course of events by mentioning that the Italians were to repeat these proposals a few weeks later in Berlin; Ambassador Alfieri, acting under instructions, reiterated them to State Secretary von Steengracht on 13 and 19 May. The stereotyped reply was characteristic of the language that Hitler's leading colleagues in the field of foreign policy thought it necessary to use at that time. Steengracht reiterated that the Russians must be beaten first. There was no doubt that this would be achieved, for 'there was only one man in Germany who could judge the situation, and that was the Führer. The impression must not be allowed to arise that we were willing to discuss peace when our policy was based on uncompromising victory.'[2]

At Klessheim Mussolini also pressed for a joint approach to Spain with a view to securing at least a right of passage for Axis troops. The reply was that the Italian government could try its luck with Franco on its own account. In this the Germans were quite right. At this stage of the war there was not the slightest prospect of securing aid or concessions from Franco.

The Italian requests for military aid were rebuffed. All they secured was a vague assurance that the possibility of reinforcing the Italian theatre with German forces and delivering weapons and equipment to the Italian army would be re-examined. But there was no prospect of even approximately meeting the requests the Italians submitted in writing. The situation in the east put this out of the question.

The position in the Balkans was discussed at length. The Italians were asked to make greater efforts in combating the partisans. There was a clash about the treatment of the Serbian nationalists, the so-called *chetniks*, whose hero and leader was Draža Mihailovich. The Germans insisted on their being crushed and disarmed, while the Italians favoured a more moderate course. They thought it desirable at least in part to play off the different rebel groups in the Balkans against one another. This would diminish the number of enemies and spare bloodshed in difficult operations in inaccessible territory. The Italians did not think much of the dubious saying 'many enemies, much honour'. They associated their military policy in the Balkans with political aims for the period after the cessation of hostilities, and in regard to the non-Communist

---

[2] A.A. Pol. Arch., Italien, Vol. 13, Nos. 124301–8 and Nos. 124356–9; Steengracht's notes of 13.5.1943 and 19.5.1943.

groups among the rebels would have liked a policy other than that of deliberate total extermination. They believed that in a later, peaceable new ordering of the Balkans it would be possible to make advantageous use of some of the nationalist groups, particularly the *chetniks*. At the back of their minds there was also the idea that detaching themselves from the ruthless German policy would help to assure their influence in these territories. Hitler had frequently and solemnly promised them such influence, but his continual interference continually cast doubt on it. The Italian attitude, always expressed very cautiously, had been made plain to me in frequent dealings with Balkan specialists in the Italian Foreign Ministry, such as Pietromarchi and Theodoli, and in conversations at the Comando Supremo with General Castellano, Colonel Mellano, and Lieutenant-Colonel Peraldo. Everyone knew that the German leadership would not hear of the idea of any kind of deal with armed groups in the Balkans where, as elsewhere, it insisted on extermination and nothing but extermination.

There is an excellent report on the matter by a German staff officer who was sent to an Italian army corps during operations in the Balkans. Colonel Ernst-Günther Baade, notwithstanding the attitude of the German High Command, stated truthfully that the Italians could not dispense with the aid of 19,000 *chetniks* in the fight against the Communists. He shared the Italian view that disarming them would merely serve to swell the partisan movement.[3]

Field-Marshal Keitel and Colonel-General Ambrosio conducted the final conversation on these Balkan questions at Klessheim. Colonel Montezemolo and I were also present. Ambrosio, in accordance with his political instructions, tried at least at one point to oppose Keitel's vigorous arguments, and made some brief proposals, that Montezemolo wrote down. I translated them for the Field-Marshal, and at this point Ribbentrop chanced to enter the room. Keitel handed him the hand-written Italian draft and asked what attitude he should take to what he called the completely inadequate Italian promises. Ribbentrop knitted his brows and began to read. I offered to translate the document for him, but with a theatrical gesture he declined. Before he could have finished it, let alone grasped its contents, he declared it to be totally unacceptable, and said he would report the matter immediately to

[3] Ktb. OKW, p. 1538.

the Führer. Then he turned and left the room, without even looking at Ambrosio. The face of the Italian general thus curtly treated was ashen, and his jaw trembled.

Thus diametrically opposite political aims again prevented any serious agreement on policy in the Balkans.

The only tangible outcome of the Klessheim meeting was the result of a proposal of Himmler's. This was that Mussolini, to bolster the Fascist régime, should build up his armed militia on the pattern of the SS, and the Germans offered to provide at short notice training personnel and modern weapons, including tanks, for a militia division, Mussolini accepted this offer to build up his Praetorian Guard. This matter was discussed at Klessheim only at the highest level, but hints filtered through. I was first told about them by Colonel Montezemolo, who asked me to give him any information that came my way, because it was doubtful whether the Comando Supremo would be kept informed about it by the party or the militia.

The conference went on for a day longer than expected, because Mussolini's state of health forced him to postpone some conversations and take to his bed. I took advantage of a free afternoon to call at the Army General Staff headquarters at the Riflemen's Barracks at Berchtesgaden. Colonel von Buttlar, Lieutenant-Colonel Boehnke, and Major von Harbou, of the operations section, asked me to brief them on the situation as it looked from Rome, and I began more or less as follows: 'If the battle in Tunisia ends in a few weeks time with a total loss of the troops, weapons, and equipment there and the North African theatre is therefore lost to us, then . . .' But that was as far as I got, because I was given the friendly advice not again to mention the theoretical possibility of a defeat in Tunisia, which might involve a dangerous charge of defeatism. I replied that in that case it would be better to talk about the weather or purely personal affairs. It was evident, however, that these officers suffered severely from being prevented by superior orders from taking foreseeable developments into account in their calculations.

Thus the Italians, particularly the soldiers, travelled back from Klessheim in a very anxious frame of mind. The fact that the problem of Tunisia had been dealt with in this way, with the consequence that there could be no practical planning for the continuation of the war in the Mediterranean area, was especially

disturbing to them. On the return journey Ambrosio was even
more reserved than usual, and for most of the time he remained in-
visible. Representatives of the Italian Foreign Ministry such as
Pietromarchi and Vitetti (who after the war became ambassador to
the O.E.E.C. in Paris) concealed their misgivings at dinner in
the train by carefully avoiding talking about anything topical.
Instead they indulged in the Italian art of telling stories.

Only one person seemed to be in better spirits on the day of the
journey back to Rome; that was Mussolini, whose pains had
diminished. Also Hitler had again impressed him and temporarily
revived his spirits.

On the day after returning to Rome I as usual gave the Minister, Prince Bismarck, and the Counsellor, Doertenbach, a full
account of what had passed. The information they were given by
Ambassador von Mackensen on these occasions was often cursory
and over-optimistic. Both had for years done their best to keep
abreast of events and moods in Italy and maintain an objective
view, which often brought them into conflict with the reports of
the ambassador, who drew his information solely from government
and party circles and as far as possible reported only what Hitler
and his entourage wanted to hear. Thus to a large extent he cut
himself off from his colleagues, with the exception of SS Obersturmbannführer Dollmann. Hence his 'lonely' reports.

Two days after returning from Klessheim, on 13 April 1943,
Alessandro Melchiori invited me to a conversation on 'neutral'
ground. Melchiori had for years been my most interesting
acquaintance among Mussolini's entourage. I had met him in
February 1941 in Tripoli, where he was officially head of the
organization that provided Italian troops with books, theatrical
entertainment, and other off-duty facilities. He wore party uniform and was a National Councillor.

On that occasion I had accompanied General Rommel on his
first memorable flight to take up his new command in Africa on
11 February 1941, and I had to help him out there for nearly two
months until all the posts on his newly-formed staff had been
filled. Melchiori therefore had an interest in maintaining contact
with me, and it was not long before I found out that Mussolini had
given him the special task of supervising and fostering the beginnings of German–Italian co-operation in Africa. He had to keep
Mussolini continually informed and report to him directly, par-

ticularly in the event of any difficulties arising. This also gave us an additional means of pushing things through when the Italian authorities in Tripoli claimed to be unable to carry out wishes expressed in Rome. General Gariboldi, the Italian commander in Tripolitania, and his staff, were, however, very receptive to Rommel's temperamental demands. Hence the Melchiori channel was used only in matters that lay outside the competence of the Italian military authorities.

Melchiori was the 'idealist' type of Fascist, and enjoyed the Duce's confidence. It turned out that Mussolini had several such men of confidence. They were free of fixed duties and kept out of the limelight, and were used for special tasks, in particular for frankly reporting on the national mood. My meetings with Melchiori in Rome generally took place at his instigation, and he generally came to my flat and only occasionally to the embassy. On a number of occasions he had given us valuable information about Mussolini's views, and in particular his increasing doubts about the outcome of the war, and he also helped us in a number of difficult situations. In 1942 his faith in the blessings of Fascism had begun to waver, and he had the courage to liberate himself from totalitarian doctrines and look at the situation realistically. Nevertheless he continued to admire Mussolini, whom he regarded as a good man. Also he wanted Italy and Germany to extricate themselves from the war on acceptable terms. It was he who among other things gave me the impressive warning contained in the Military Attaché's report of 12 March 1943 quoted above, namely that the radical and anti-Church developments taking place in Germany were repugnant to his fellow-countrymen, including convinced Fascists, and were seriously affecting German–Italian relations.

When we met on 13 April 1943, the subject of our discussion was the outcome of the Klessheim talks, of which Mussolini had already informed him. The interesting thing that he told me was that Mussolini had again succumbed to deep disillusionment; representations by his political and military advisers had destroyed the illusions that Hitler had given him. He was particularly distressed at the idea that Hitler imagined he had talked him out of the idea that the Russian campaign must be brought to an end. He still believed that to be the only way of bringing about a tolerable end of the war.

Loss of North Africa

The weeks after the Klessheim meeting corresponded with the final stages of the fighting in Tunisia. German and Italian troops had been sent there in November 1942; the first landings had been improvised, but a continual stream of reinforcements had followed. This operation took place shortly after Rommel's army had been forced to retreat after the battle of El Alamein and the Americans landed in Algeria. According to traditional General Staff doctrine, the German–Italian landing in Tunisia could have only two possible objectives:

1. To cover the retreat of Rommel's army, and simultaneously to make possible the transport back to Italy of as large a proportion as possible of the Axis forces that were being squeezed in western Libya and Tunisia before they were finally crushed by a massive allied pincer movement from east and west. In the face of allied air and naval supremacy in the Mediterranean, no military expert could believe in the possibility of a lasting defence, let alone offensive operations, in the face of the continual and unhampered reinforcement of the allied armies in the North African theatre. The conditions under which a bridgehead can be held are taught in the military academies of all the countries of the world, and these were non-existent in Tunisia from the outset.

2. To gain time for defensive preparations against a later allied invasion of the Italian islands and mainland. But, as it was forbidden by order of the German leadership to take into account the possibility that Tunisia might be lost, only inadequate preparations and troop movements were made.

A retrospective note at the end of the war diary of the German High Command mentions that this situation should have been taken into account.[4]

Hitler was partly influenced by the idea that the objective of gaining time that had dominated German–Italian operations on all fronts since 1942 also served for the development of 'miracle weapons'. He also nourished illusions that the enemy alliance would break up during the war. This too made the gaining of time an urgent necessity. Hence he tried to extend to North Africa his disastrous principle that not an inch of ground must be yielded anywhere and that the last soldier's life must be sacrificed even in hopeless situations.

[4] Ibid., pp. 1603–9.

Field-Marshal Kesselring states in his memoirs[5] that, as the responsible Supreme Commander South, he still counted seriously on the possibility of holding out in the African theatre at this time. He admits that after the American landing the German–Italian troops were besieged in a huge fortress, but in the spring of 1943 he still wanted to use these forces for offensive operations. From time to time he actually planned attacks on an apparently substantial scale. Nevertheless for years past he must have seen for himself that, after the vital mistake made at the beginning of the operations, namely the failure to seize Malta, British air and naval supremacy in the Mediterranean made it impossible to send adequate reinforcements and supplies to Africa. He was just as well aware that at the time of the fighting in Tunisia the transport situation had become even more disastrous, because now the American air force intervened, Tunis was the only harbour left to us, and our shipping had been reduced to a minimum.

This optimism of Field-Marshal Kesselring's marked the whole conduct of the war in the Mediterranean area. He displays his optimistic nature in his memoirs. Of the operations in Sicily, for instance, he writes: 'In spite of the obvious progress of the allies in the conduct of the war, a manifestly hopeless situation was not necessarily irremediable.'[6] Even Hitler called him a 'colossal optimist'.[7]

The same optimism, however, frequently crops up in Hitler's letters to Mussolini when he talks about the prospects in North Africa without any first-hand knowledge. A good example is provided by the following passage from the letter of 14 March 1943.[8] 'If, Duce, we succeed in holding the Mareth position, or at worst at least the Chott position, and bring the convoy system into good order, no power in the world will be able to throw us out of North Africa.' A few lines later he says: 'If we succeed in getting the supply position into good shape I do not doubt that sooner or later the British and American North African adventure will turn out to be their most disastrous mistake.'

Kesselring writes angrily in his book about Ambrosio, who had been Chief of the Comando Supremo since the beginning of 1943.[9] The two were in fact soldiers of very different stamp, and frictionless co-operation between them was hardly to be expected. As

---

[5] Kesselring, p. 203 f.   [6] Ibid., p. 227.   [7] Warlimont, p. 338.
[8] A.A. Pol. Arch., RAM–Film, F10229–32.   [9] Kesselring, p. 228 f.

Ambrosio played an important part in the dramatic events of July and August 1943, a brief personal description seems desirable. He originally served in the Italian cavalry, and both his sons were cavalry officers. I had been able to observe him closely in 1941 and 1942 at conferences at the Army General Staff, of which he was chief until he took over the Comando Supremo.

He created the impression of being serious and reserved; super-ficially he might seem actually sulky. His statements and argu-ments always had a striking clarity; they revealed a cool, calculat-ing intelligence. He did not possess the Italian wealth of gesture; on the contrary, his manner and bearing were much more like those attributed to German and particularly Prussian staff officers of the old school. The Piedmontese have often been called the Prussians of Italy, and Ambrosio came from Piedmont; he was born in Turin in 1879. His personality inspired me with liking and respect.

Closer acquaintance revealed the passionate nature that was held in check by his self-control. He was deeply disturbed about his country's future, because his clear intelligence permitted him no illusions about the inadequacy of its resources. His sense of responsibility drove him continually to seek for ways out. His atti-tude to the German ally was that of most of the Italian generals. They had the greatest admiration for the valour and training of the German troops, for German generalship on the field of battle, for the German talent for organization, and for the German arma-ments industry. However, the campaign in Russia, and in par-ticular the African campaign, caused them to have doubts about the German strategic leadership. Above all, they increasingly came to believe that German leadership in the Mediterranean area had failed because it was unused to combined sea, air, and land opera-tions. The German commanders were not familiar with the special laws applying to long lines of communication oversea, for their training and experience applied only to continental warfare. The Italian General Staff therefore deplored the fact that on strategic matters Mussolini nearly always gave in to Hitler's pressure and left too much responsibility to the Germans.

I, too, as a result of attending numerous conferences about operations in the Mediterranean area, came to the conclusion that Italian proposals for oversea warfare were more realistic and promising of success. I am sure that this will be confirmed by war

historians' assessments of all the circumstances. But it was the
German leadership that had its way, and it was the German assessments and plans that were acted on. The Italian generals were well
aware that in the last resort the decision lay with Adolf Hitler, and
they noted bitterly that the Führer issued his orders from Rasten-
burg in East Prussia or from Berchtesgaden, and that throughout
the war neither he, nor Field-Marshal Keitel, nor Göring, the
chief of the Luftwaffe, nor General Jodl, nor any of the various
German Army Chiefs of Staff paid a single visit to any of the fronts
in the Mediterranean area to gain a personal impression. German
military tradition can show better examples of close contact
between High Command and troops in the field. Field-Marshal
Kesselring provided such an example. He continually flew across
the Mediterranean to formations in the forward areas, and in
many dangerous situations showed himself to be a model un-
daunted commander. His friendly and understanding manner
towards the Italians won him a great deal of confidence. But his
unjustified optimism in the vital phases of the war in 1943 brought
him up against the stern sense of reality of Colonel-General
Ambrosio.

In view of the testing time that lay ahead, General von Rintelen
made continual efforts to mediate. The military prospects were
black in any case, but the political prospects made it seem essential
that Field-Marshal Kesselring should remain at his post for, if he
were relieved, it was to be feared that Hitler would replace him by
someone lacking the qualities necessary for dealing with fine-
nerved allies. It also seemed essential that no difficulties should be
put in the way of Ambrosio's remaining at his post as a result of
dissension with his German colleagues. Because of his sense of
responsibility and the strength of his position in the Italian officers'
corps, he could certainly be regarded as an authentic representative of his country.

On 8 June 1943 Rintelen gave a dinner party for Kesselring and
Ambrosio, attended by fourteen guests. Here again it was evident
to the observer how little there was in common between the German Supreme Commander South, who was likeable but excessively set on radiating unshakable confidence, and the Chief of the
Comando Supremo, who trusted only in facts and figures. The
evening brought them no closer.

After the collapse in Tunisia in the middle of May 1943, Colonel-

General Ambrosio and his colleagues, among whom General Roatta, the uncommonly acute Chief of the Army General Staff, deserves especial mention, had to face the prospect of an invasion bringing the war on to Italian soil.

In a full report dated 6 May 1943 that again was drafted by me, Rintelen again gave warning of the situation that would arise after the loss of Africa. Once more it was circumstantially pointed out that the Italian army had intervened in 1940 inadequately armed and equipped for modern warfare and had therefore been condemned to suffer one setback after another on all fronts. Attention was also drawn to other deficiencies—in training, organization, and in lower and mid-level leadership. Thorough-going reforms while the war was in progress were hampered by lack of raw materials and insufficient enthusiasm for the Italian cause among wide circles. The Fascist slogans 'Italy a great power' and *mare nostrum* had never made any real impact. The repercussion of all the Italian defeats, and now the prospect of the invasion of their country, which was unprepared for defence, had caused the morale of the population to sink to an all-time low. The remaining Italian military formations could be regarded only as weak stop-gaps in the positions of their German ally.

The following phrases of this report are significant:

The Italian army has a large number of very sharp-witted generals and admirals fit for the command of formations of large and the largest sizes. Had they been able to establish the corresponding formations, the situation of the Italian army would be very different.[10]

The superficial and often corrupt Fascist leadership was responsible for the fact that even the limited amount of war material that the country was capable of producing was not made available to the Italian troops. For years Italian officers had looked enviously at the admirable equipment of the German armed forces, and this was yet another reason why most of them rejected the Fascist régime. Dislike turned gradually to hate, and tension between troops and Blackshirts grew. This made a substantial contribution to the undermining of Fascism.

General von Rintelen submitted another report, dated 26 May 1943, that Deakin[11] describes as a 'masterly summary' and 'a penetrating study of the Italian problem'.

[10] Own notes, and Deakin, p. 283.   [11] Deakin, p. 361 f.

After the loss of Tunisia, German–Italian co-operation loped into a tug-of-war for German reinforcements for the coming battle for Sicily, Sardinia, and the Italian mainland. The Comando Supremo drew up long lists showing the numbers of German divisions, Luftwaffe formations, and anti-aircraft units required. It also enumerated the weapons and items of equipment needed by the Italian troops, and asked for numerous tank and anti-tank units to bolster the Italian divisions. The German command was also asked to agree to the withdrawal of more Italian divisions from the Balkans and the south of France.

Mussolini hesitated. He was not anxious to have so many German troops on Italian soil, and he dreamed of defending his country principally with Italian troops. Also he was reluctant to withdraw any substantial number of Italian troops from other theatres, because he wanted Italy to be seen to be continuing its contribution to pan-European warfare. The Italian generals, and leading Fascists as well, consequently began to have doubts about the dictator's mental condition; there was no doubt about the deterioration of his physical condition.

He ended by partially giving in, at any rate in regard to the appeal for German reinforcements. Some of the requests, particularly for Luftwaffe aid, were met to a very limited extent, but the German High Command declared them as a whole to be exaggerated and unfulfillable. It objected most strongly to the idea of sending ten German divisions to Italy; General Roatta in particular had repeatedly and persistently declared aid on that scale to be indispensable,[12] but Mussolini and the Comando Supremo were informed in a number of letters, notes, and verbal communications that the idea was Utopian. The negotiations for these divisions had notable repercussions later, that is to say, after 25 July.

To us in Rome the question presented itself as follows. In the first place, it was clear that, if there was to be any prospect of an at least temporarily successful defence, Roatta's demand, which was supported by Ambrosio, was militarily completely justified. On the other hand, so far as we could judge the situation on other fronts, German High Command's view that it was impossible to spare so many divisions was equally justified. But we felt entitled to suspect that Hitler himself was reckoning on the possibility of an

[12] Ktb. OKW, p. 1447 f.

Italian military collapse. The reports of the Military Attaché that we have quoted must have suggested this to him, and no doubt he considered it dangerous to commit so many divisions to Italy, and anxiety on this score was strengthened by the view then being taken by the German High Command that the allies might land in northern Italy, perhaps in the Leghorn area. This would put all German troops farther south in a dangerous position. This merry-go-round of considerations necessarily created suspicion between Germans and Italians. The Germans did not want to commit too many troops to a doubtful situation, and therefore declared them to be unavailable. The Italians, however, were concerned with the defence of their country, and sober military opinion was that in the absence of these reinforcements it was indefensible. At the same time the Italians noted that the German High Command committed itself to the defence of Sicily with a display of confidence and at least half measures. When the probable time for the allied invasion of southern Europe from Libya and Tunisia drew close, the German High Command decided at least to send a few divisions piecemeal to Italy, though units in need of rest and replenishment were among them. When the arrival of each unit was announced, the German High Command solemnly declared that it was the last that could be spared for the Mediterranean area.

Meanwhile the arms and equipment for an armoured militia division that had been promised at the Klessheim meeting were punctually delivered, and Germans were sent to conduct a course of training that was to be completed by the middle of July.

This led to a ticklish incident. On 1 May 1943, that is, three weeks after the meeting between Hitler, Himmler, and Mussolini at Klessheim, a teleprinter message from the Supreme Commander South landed on my desk saying that in the course of the month thirty-six tanks and a number of 8·8-cm. anti-aircraft guns were arriving in Italy for delivery to the Italians. This was one of the usual messages announcing the forthcoming arrival of arms or equipment for the Italians, which we always passed on to the Comando Supremo without comment. After the confidential information given to me at Klessheim by Colonel Montezemolo, it was evident that this delivery could be intended only for Mussolini's militia. But, as I had no official knowledge of the arrangement, I gave myself the pleasure of carrying out my friend Montezemolo's request that I should keep him informed about future

developments in connection with this matter. I laid the information on his desk at the Comando Supremo the same day.

Four days later SS Sturmführer Wenner, a subordinate of Dollmann's, appeared in my office and wanted to know whether I had passed on to the Italians any message about the delivery of special weapons. I explained that I had no knowledge of any special deliveries, but that all messages about forthcoming delivery of supplies of any kind were automatically passed on to the Comando Supremo, in accordance with procedure that had been established for many years. I told him that, if he had any particular case in mind and would give me details, I should be happy to make inquiries, but he declined this offer and stalked out of the office in an obvious state of irritation.

On 8 May Colonel von Buttlar telephoned me from the Army General Staff and told me rather excitedly that on the previous day at the funeral of Lutze, the SA Chief of Staff, Himmler had complained to Hitler about me. He said I had tried to 'divert' to the Italian army German arms deliveries confidentially intended for the Italian militia, and that an investigation of the case had already been ordered.

When General von Rintelen was ordered to report on the matter soon afterwards, he was able to reply perfectly truthfully that he had no instructions that information about arms deliveries was not to be passed on to the Italians in any particular case.

Apart from the permanent addiction of the highest German authorities of the time to seeking out culprits, the attempt to keep deliveries of weapons to the militia secret for a time was exceedingly naïve. On 10 July 1943 Mussolini inspected the new armoured militia division north of Rome, and representatives of the Comando Supremo were invited to the ceremony. So they then had an opportunity to count the weapons the delivery of which was already known to them from the information passed on to Montezemolo at the beginning of May.

Waiting for the Invasion

At the beginning of July there was growing tension and nervousness in Rome at the prospect of an allied invasion. The population sensed the goshawk hovering over the ill-protected chicken-run. Air raids on the big cities with the exception of Rome grew bigger

c

and more frequent. Also the food situation was causing anxiety. Leading party personalities issued ardent and often contradictory appeals, announcing new measures in all fields, but people only smiled at them. Everyone knew that defeat would mean the end of Fascism. Most opponents of the régime consoled themselves for the anxieties of the immediate future with that thought. What everyone wanted was a quick end to it all, and without too many horrors.

When the German Embassy was called on to report on the mood in Rome, the ferment among the people, and likely political developments, it was in a difficult position. Ambassador von Mackensen, supported and supervised by Dollmann, held fast to his line. When he occasionally mentioned ominous developments that could no longer be overlooked, he nevertheless declared the position of Mussolini and the Fascist hierarchy to be solid as a rock, and said that their loyalty to the German alliance was unshakable. He drew his information almost exclusively from representatives of the government and high party officials, and he had always scrupulously avoided contact with circles and individuals whose attitude to Fascism was sceptical, and his sources were therefore very defective. He either refused to believe worrying news brought him by his colleagues or minimized it in his reports.

A striking example of his views of the situation is provided by a telegram dated 21 May 1943, that is, a fortnight after the fall of Tunisia.[13] He admitted that the popular mood was depressed as a result of the military situation and food-supply difficulties. But the development of this grave situation had strengthened the circles that 'because of their deepest convictions hold fast to the necessity of holding out until joint final victory'. The changes and purges in the party, he said, were apparently already yielding positive results; thus, in spite of all signs of crisis, it was not yet too late for a change for the better. In contrast to the intellectual top strata in the cities, particularly in Rome, the spirit of the masses would enable the Duce to kindle a determined spirit of resistance, just as at the end of the First World War the collapse at Caporetto had been followed by an Italian victory. 'Because of their lack of substance, there is no need to go into rumours relating to a crisis between the Duce, the supreme army leadership, and the Royal House.'

[13] A.A. Pol. Arch., Italien, Vol. 13, No. 124377.

Apart from the first sentence, everything in this statement was wrong. The gravest mistake was drawing a distinction between the attitude to the war situation of the 'top strata' and the 'mass of the people' in Italy. This was bound to lead to false prognoses.

I have often wondered what caused Ambassador von Mackensen to adopt this attitude, particularly as after the Italian collapse it earned him nothing but ingratitude from his government. His dignified appearance and his amiability, though he showed the latter only in off-duty contacts, were attractive. Also in more intimate circles he could be really humorous. To foreigners, however, he always seemed too stiff and unapproachable, even when he made efforts to be friendly. The basis of his character was a rigid loyalty to principles. He often spoke of his time as an officer in the Foot Guards, and it may have been from that part of his career that he derived a sense of duty that was too rigid for his later responsibilities, preventing him from ever diverging from a line of march on which he had once set out. Perhaps he believed he owed this to the Guards' motto, *semper talis*. This principle determined his conduct and made him suppress doubts when they arose. But it is unintelligible that he should actually have courted an individual with whom he had as little in common as Dollmann, Himmler's representative in Rome, and above all accepted his advice.

In this connection we may quote what is said about him by Guariglia, who became Foreign Minister in Badoglio's government and had known him for many years in Rome and Madrid. He says in his memoirs: 'Mackensen was permeated by a sense of absolute discipline and hence a ruthless sense of duty, though inwardly he had no sympathy for Nazism and, particularly in August 1943, had not much confidence about the outcome of the war'.[14]

Prince Bismarck, the Minister, and Doertenbach, the Counsellor at the Embassy, were often put in a dilemma by their chief's behaviour. They maintained in exemplary fashion a wide range of contacts with all individuals and groups who were important for forming a view. Since the beginning of their work in Rome they had been in close contact with always very well-informed circles belonging to so-called Roman society, which was very concerned with maintaining independence of outlook in Italy. Information coming from these circles yielded a far more accurate picture of the

[14] Guariglia, p. 610.

situation and prospects at any particular time than purely official contacts.

General von Rintelen, apart from his excellent relations with all the important Italian generals, had gained himself a very respected situation in Rome society. In spite of the war, the situation was such that it was in the interests of the Military Attaché and his aides that they should cultivate contacts of this kind. This resulted in insights the value of which far exceeded that of information gathered in the course of official calls. In the houses in which one met the Colonnas, the Ruspolis, the Torlonias, and among the mass of the people, one met the Italian reality that Fascism could not alter but was obstinately disbelieved in in Germany.

These social relations also involved contact with the diplomatic representatives of neutral states and states allied to Germany. This continually provided favourable opportunities for testing and supplementing one's picture of the situation.

I had the good fortune of being able to confirm from my own experience how useful off-duty interests, whether in the field of music, sport, or anything else, can be for the creation and cultivation of contacts that turn out to be an invaluable aid in carrying out one's official duties. I quickly developed friendly relations, for instance, with Italians who knew that in 1939 I had been a candidate for selection for the equestrian events in the next Olympic Games. I met the well-known Italian horsemen Conforti and Count Bettoni, Major Filliponi, the commander of the riding school at Tor di Quinto outside the gates of Rome, Bonivento and Chiantia, who competed in the Olympic Games of 1936, and the great horse-lovers Calzavara and Alvisi. Meetings with them and their wide circle of friends led automatically to frank conversations, and consequently to valuable knowledge of conditions and feelings in the host country.

The reserved attitude of the ambassador necessarily led early to close co-operation between Bismarck and Rintelen, and Doertenbach and I were drawn in too. The background to this was agreement in political outlook and identity of view about conditions in Italy and the military prospects. We were united by the belief that the true and better Italy was to be found in circles in which the methods of the Fascist government were being subjected to increasing criticism.

Bismarck and Doertenbach maintained close contact with us in

order to keep abreast of the military situation, and the Military Attaché's continual contact with the Comando Supremo and his many contacts with Italian officers yielded invaluable information.

This daily exchange of ideas had already resulted in 1941 and 1942 in a strange game of to-and-fro in the drafting of embassy reports. Political reports were signed by the ambassador, and it was only rarely that Bismarck was able to secure inclusion in them of observations and conclusions the frankness of which would have caused displeasure in Berlin. Bismarck therefore often submitted the offending drafts for inclusion in the Military Attaché's reports. These had to be submitted to the ambassador for signature, but he was not allowed to make any changes in them; he could only add his own comments or dissociate himself from them. When Bismarck acted as Chargé d'Affaires in the ambassador's absence, the Embassy reports were freer in their language and often took into account the Military Attaché's impressions.

Looking at the Foreign Ministry documents today, it is noticeable, for instance, that during the ambassador's absence on the occasion of the Klessheim meeting in April 1943 Prince Bismarck passed on very serious news about the popular mood in Sicily, to which the ambassador would certainly not have put his signature.

In this connection a memorandum by Prince Bismarck dated 27 December 1940 is worth mentioning. Under the impact of the setbacks the Italians had just suffered in Greece and North Africa, the writer, correctly interpreting all the circumstances and symptoms, already went so far as to speak of the danger that the war in the Mediterranean area might be lost. Ambassador von Mackensen, who had asked his Minister to draft the memorandum, did not pass it on, but had it put in the files.[15]

Of the many evenings I spent and the earnest conversations I had at Prince Bismarck's house, there is one occasion on 3 July 1943 that stands out in my memory. Herr Gisevius, who was later involved in the 20 July 1944 plot to assassinate Hitler, and is the author of the book *To the Bitter End*, had come to Rome from Switzerland, and Prince Bismarck invited my wife and me to spend the evening with him. Princess Bismarck happened not to be in Rome at the time. The four of us discussed the gloomy prospects until late at night. After dinner Prince Bismarck dismissed all

[15] ADAP, D, Vol. XI, 2, p. 819.

the servants and checked from time to time to make sure that no one was listening behind the closed doors to the neighbouring rooms.

Gisevius told us about his conspiratorial activities, but could not confirm the hope that an attempt might soon be made in Germany to end the war by internal resistance. He praised the activity of civilian groups, without mentioning names, but expressed disappointment at the hesitations of the generals. He said that, with luck, imminent events in Italy might act as a spur and increase the strength of the resistance movement in Germany. German army and army group commanders might then, perhaps, allow themselves to be convinced that for Germany the hands of the clock were remorselessly moving forward to five minutes to twelve.

Gisevius wanted to know what we could tell him about anti-Fascist activity in Italy. We were able to quote many examples of Italian opposition to Fascism and the continuation of the war. We knew that at least half the leading Fascist personalities were expecting an upheaval. But we also believed that, in accordance with the Italian temperament, practically all these opponents of the régime had excessively individual ideas about overthrowing Fascism and bringing the war to an end. In 1943 we could see no signs of the gathering of organized resistance or the formation of action groups. But we had reason to believe that a number of personalities in public life and in the party were trying to spin conspiratorial threads, and that many generals were hoping for a political change of scene. We also knew from frequent hints by Italian friends that they looked to the monarchy as a point of support in the crises and ordeals that lay ahead.

Filippo Anfuso, Mussolini's last ambassador in Berlin, describes in his memoirs how it became almost a social 'must' in Italy to be a small or medium conspirator, particularly if one occupied a post of more than average importance.[16] He calls all this activity 'conspiracy in cells'. A small number of like-minded people would remain together for a time, but would then switch to other 'cells'. But soon they would discover another group that had a different answer to the problem of rescuing the nation from calamity. In this confusing multitude of dissatisfied individuals and cells, all deeply concerned about their country's fate, the only thing that was lacking was the most important thing of all, that is, a unifying

[16] Anfuso, p. 219 f.

idea. This conspiratorial mood that gradually became universal could be compared with semitone music played by an orchestra without a conductor.

At no time in the war was the expression of opinion in Italy restricted to anything like the extent that it was in Germany. Political sarcasm was freely expressed in Rome society, but it could not be inferred from this that an upheaval was being deliberately planned. All revolutionary impulses were paralysed by the country's dependence on its far stronger and highly determined ally. Resistance to Hitler's amateurish and irresponsible leadership, resistance prepared to take planned action, developed in terrorized Germany years earlier than it did among the Italian people, which was much more gently treated under Fascism. But criticism was not dangerous in Italy, the Italians were used to it, and consequently, when the day of revolt or reckoning came, they were better prepared to follow those willing to take the initiative. This was also encouraged by eager listening to the allied radio, which was generally not attended with risk.

During those summer months the current phrase in Rome was: *È giunta l'ora?* ('Has the hour come?') The question would be asked with a mocking smile whenever anyone came across a group engaged in lively discussion. It would be asked if a baby suddenly screamed, or if there was an unusual noise outside in the street. It would be asked by one's host if one had to put off an invitation at short notice. It was the expression of a conviction arising from a still secret sense of resistance that something was bound to happen very soon. The cavalry captain Sandri Poli asked it when his groom failed to turn up with our horses at the riding grounds on the Pincio one morning. He thought a state of emergency might have kept the man in the barracks.

Our cook, the admirable Maria, the daughter of a Tuscan peasant, gave us graphic descriptions of the mood in the market-place without ever being asked for them. The government and the war were daily cursed aloud there a thousand times a day, and the police on duty never lifted a finger. Maria used to refer to Signor Mussolini as *il fetente* ('the stinker'), and I would reprovingly wag my finger at her when she used such disrespectful language, but she refused to give up this token of her solidarity with opinion in the streets and in the market-place. In normal times I should have had to get rid of her, for toleration of such drastic derogation of the

head of her government in the house of a foreigner who was on the diplomatic list might have led to disagreeable consequences.

Fighting in Sicily and the Feltre meeting

The second great amphibious operation carried out by the allies in the Second World War began on the night of 9–10 July 1943. Forces equipped with every modern device landed at several points on the south coast of Sicily. The guns of heavy naval units laid down an effective barrage round the landing-places, making the bringing up of local reserves by the defence uncommonly difficult. The German–Italian air defence, which was too weak in any case, was helpless against the hail of fire from the ships. The British and Americans had so perfected the arming of their warships with long-range anti-aircraft guns that an accurate approach by attacking aircraft was almost impossible. The successes against heavy naval units achieved by aircraft in the early war years could no longer be repeated. At this stage the technique of warfare had taken a turn that favoured the navy.

On the morning of 10 July Mussolini carried out his long-announced inspection of the armoured militia division north of Rome. His state of health was liable to continual ups and downs, and on this occasion he looked reasonably spry again. He clambered about very nimbly in one of the new German tanks, but the news from Sicily that was continually brought him caused his eyes to have an unsteady look.

By 11 July it was evident that the landings had been successful. As a result of the great inferiority of their weapons and the deterioration in their morale, the Italian troops on the coast put up no resistance worthy of the name. When the German Hermann Göring Division, which was the backbone of the reserve, moved forward from the interior of the island, it was repeatedly held up by damage done to the narrow roads by enemy air attacks, and it was therefore unable to deliver a counter-blow in good time at the especially threatened landing-place near Gela. But even apart from these circumstances, the relation of forces as a whole offered no prospect of a successful defence against these landings.

In the first few days of the fighting the question whether it was worth while sending more German and Italian troops to Sicily made even Field-Marshal Kesselring hesitate. Hitler and

Mussolini announced officially that the island must be held, and that the allies were going to suffer a great defeat there. So a delaying action was fought, and some German and Italian troops were sent across.

Mussolini sent Hitler one appeal after another, asking for more German reinforcements, particularly by the Luftwaffe. The Comando Supremo did the same by way of the official channels to the German High Command. Some aid was always promised, but it was always too little. Words of comfort, good advice, and moral encouragement were also sent. Thus Ribbentrop on 15 July instructed the German Ambassador by telegram to inform Scorza, the party secretary, who also appealed for aid, that 'all our thoughts and wishes at this time are with the Italian people and the Fascist Party, on which Italy's fate for the future depends'.[17]

German–Italian relations during the fortnight from 10 July to 25 July are characterized as follows by Dino Alfieri, the Italian Ambassador in Berlin, in a dispatch to Bastianini, the Under-Secretary of State, dated 14 July:

Germany is completely absorbed by the operations against Soviet Russia, against which she is still nourishing plans for large-scale offensives. With that in view she intends to conserve her forces as far as possible, raise new ones, and prevent any attack on Reich territory as long as possible. Hence she regards neighbouring allied and occupied territories as bastions of the German fortress. . . . One has the impression that Germany is endeavouring to prolong the heroic resistance of Italy at limited cost.[18]

That is what all responsible Italians, and in particular the senior military commanders, were saying during those weeks. Concern for their country's fate led gradually to a mood of desperation. The developments that were to follow were thus foreshadowed in advance. During this period Colonel-General Ambrosio submitted to Mussolini the draft of a telegram to Hitler that contained the phrase: 'The primary purpose of the sacrifice of my country cannot be that of delaying a direct attack on Germany.'[19] The war diary of the German High Command actually states that the continuation of the struggle on Italian soil was directed to keeping the

[17] A.A. Pol. Arch., Italien, Vol. 14, No. 72400.
[18] Dino Alfieri, *Due dittatori di fronte*, Milan, 1951, p. 298 f.
[19] Deakin, p. 379.

war as far as possible away from the 'heart of Europe and thus from the German frontiers'.[20]

A few days after the beginning of the fighting in Sicily, Prince Philip of Hesse, the son-in-law of the King of Italy, came to Rome. He had often made himself available for special missions in regard to German–Italian co-operation, and had already done so in the years before the war. Ambassador von Mackensen asked me to join them for a stroll in the embassy garden so that I could state my view of the situation in Sicily. When I had finished, the prince asked me how long Sicily could be held, and on the basis of continuous study of the situation and my knowledge of all the messages it was not difficult to hazard the prediction that it might be able to hold out for four or five weeks. Mackensen leant back and looked at me reprovingly behind the prince's back. Thirty days later Sicily was completely in allied hands.

In the early stages of the operations in Sicily the illusion occasionally arose that the British and Americans would run into supply difficulties, and that by stubbornly fighting for time a turnabout in the situation might yet be achieved. This hope was nourished by German sources. On 7 May 1943 State Secretary von Steengracht assured Galbiati, the chief of the Italian militia, on a visit to Berlin, that if the allies landed in Europe shortage of shipping and supplies would create grave difficulties for them after three or at most six weeks.[21] Unfortunately the German naval command often had such ideas about the American shipping potential. By way of contrast, I recall Prince Bismarck's ironical comment that it was regrettable that it was impossible to arrange a brief tour of the arsenals of American industry, now converted to war production, for the Reich government and the German commanders, because that would quickly rid them of their illusions.

The shock of the successful allied landing in Sicily caused the plan for another meeting between Hitler and Mussolini, which had been discussed for several weeks, to take place at short notice at Feltre in Upper Italy on 19 July.

At this meeting Hitler had two aims. He wanted yet again to spur Mussolini and the Italian generals to increased efforts, and he also wanted to form an idea of how justified were the doubts that had now arisen about how long Italy would hold out on the German side.

[20] Ktb. OKW, p. 832.   [21] A.A. Pol. Arch., Italien, Vol. 13, No. 124265.

Mussolini went to Feltre hoping for advice, consolation and, above all, aid from his friend Hitler.

Three days before, on 16 July, fifteen party leaders had secured his consent to an early meeting of the Grand Council of the Fascist Party, but this at first remained unknown on the German side.

The Grand Council had not met since 1939. It was now to meet in a few days' time to discuss the fate of the country and the party and consider new measures.

Before going to Feltre, Mussolini was subjected to even stronger pressure by the Comando Supremo. Colonel-General Ambrosio insisted that he should tell Hitler in all frankness that Italy was at the end of her tether. The Germans must now be asked for binding declarations about adequate reinforcements, with commitment to exact dates. The necessity for immediate action was self-evident in view of the fact that fighting was now taking place on Italian soil, and nothing but immediate action would do.

Colonel-General Ambrosio's representations were based on a dramatic memorandum by the Comando Supremo drafted on 14 July, four days after the allied landing in Sicily. As the contents of this document are important for the whole course of subsequent events, including the Italian withdrawal from the war on the German side, we shall reproduce it in full. A copy of the Italian original came into the hands of the German High Command soon after the capitulation of the Badoglio government on 8 September 1943.

In February 1944 I was asked by the German High Command for an assessment of this document, because it had been suggested that it was possible to conclude from it that on 14 July Italy had already decided to abandon the 'Axis alliance'. I could not accept this view. The insistence that the 'centre of gravity of operations' should be shifted against 'the most dangerous enemy at present, the Anglo-Americans', and that the formation of a permanent second front should be crushed in the bud, were evidence against it. The fact that the document as a whole stated the existing dangers in full with all their implications testified to its author's sense of responsibility. In the dangerous situation that had also been admitted by leaders of the party, the fact that the ominous last paragraph called for energetic decisions by the political leadership must be regarded as flowing from the supreme commander's sense of duty. It would therefore be frivolous to suggest that by

this memorandum Ambrosio had merely wanted to absolve himself of further responsibility. The fact that he asked to be relieved of his post[22] on 20 July, the day after the conversation at Feltre, showed the opposite. The following is translated from the rather lame German High Command translation, a copy of which I received in February 1944:

14 July 1944 XXI[23]

Appreciation of the Situation in the event of the Loss of Sicily.

I. The fate of Sicily must be regarded as sealed, whether in the long or short term.

The essential reasons for this swift defeat are:

The complete lack of counter-action by us at sea and weak resistance in the air during the enemy's approach to the coast, the landing and the enemy's penetration and our counter-attacks.

The inadequacy of the armament and composition of the coast divisions, the small number and capacity of resistance of the defensive positions, the small fighting strength (armament) and mobility of the Italian field divisions.

There is no point in reiterating the reasons for the state of affairs; it is the result of three years of war begun with slender resources. During this time our limited resources and strength were used up in Africa, Russia, and the Balkans. The same difficult circumstances exist in Sardinia, Corsica, and the whole peninsula.

II. After the capture of Sicily the following possibilities for further action will lie open to the enemy:

(*a*) Methodical action against the Italian mainland (co-ordinated series of single operations within fighter range from south and north); or a single operation aimed at cutting the peninsula in two.

(*b*) Using Sardinia and Corsica as stepping-stones for an operation against the peninsula, or the coast of Provence.

The first alternative (action against the peninsula) is the more probable, because it seems unlikely that Sicily would be attacked for the purpose of gaining Leghorn, Genoa, or Toulon, with the prospect of having to carry out three successive landings instead of two.

In none of these eventualities, however, are we in a position to cope with the situation, for

1. After the Sicilian experience, our air and sea inferiority make the problem insoluble in the case of Sardinia and Corsica, even if improvements and reinforcements could be expected.

---

[22] Vanna Vailati, *Badoglio racconta*, Turin, 1956, p. 363. Rintelen, p. 215.

[23] The 'XXI' after the date indicated, in accordance with the usual practice under the Fascist régime, the number of years that had passed since its establishment in 1922.

2. Defence of the peninsula requires a tremendous amount of material as well as army and air strength that we cannot raise by ourselves.

If the above-mentioned material and forces cannot be delivered, the gradual loss of the whole peninsula must be expected, with the consequent impossibility of continuing to supply the Italian forces in the Balkans and the Aegean.

Hence the necessity must be faced of introducing German army and air forces into Italy (armoured corps, and more than those already transferred to Italy, and 2,000 aircraft) even at the price of a temporary suspension of operations in the east, in order to defend Italy and win back relative mastery of the air in the Mediterranean.

From the above there follow:

The necessity for the Axis of shifting the centre of gravity of operations against the most dangerous enemy, at present the Anglo-Americans who, if they occupied the Italian peninsula, would be in a position to strike a vital blow at the Balkans (Rumanian oil);

The urgency on principle of crushing in the bud the formation of a permanent second land front, as in the longer or shorter term the Anglo-Americans would succeed in gaining absolute superiority on such a second front.

III. The so slender Italian possibilities of naval resistance that we have here described, which were plainly shown up by the enemy during recent operations, may induce him to accelerate the pace of his operations. Hence the immediate withdrawal of the above-mentioned forces to Italy is indispensable.

With our own resources alone we shall be able to fight, but only with such meagre results that they will not suffice even to rescue our military honour in the face of the world.

On the other hand our ally cannot persuade us that possibilities of victory still exist for the Axis if the formation of a second land front in Europe is not prevented while the war in Russia lasts.

If the formation of this front cannot be prevented, it is the duty of the highest political authorities to consider whether it is not advisable and necessary to spare the country further grief and ruins and anticipate the end of the struggle, because the final result would no doubt be still worse one or more years later.

In the light of this document let us return to the conversations at Feltre on 19 July 1943. Mussolini had undertaken to talk to Hitler in the way demanded of him.

It will always be difficult for historians to explain why Mussolini, in spite of this double pressure, both political and military, ignored the vital interests of his country at Feltre. For two hours he

listened to Hitler's usual monologue. The latter conjured up the past, spoke long-windedly of the importance of raw materials for the conduct of modern warfare, exalted the art of improvisation and, above all, the value of Nazi and Fascist ideas.

He described the potentialities of American armament production as limited, because of the excessive specialization of American industry. As against this, excellent prospects would be opening up to the German war leadership in the immediate future. Expanded production of improved aircraft and tanks had already begun, and Germany would soon be very successful again in the U-boat war. The building of U-boats was now being accelerated, and they were being provided with new devices that would make their detection by the enemy more difficult. Before the end of the coming winter new weapons against which there was no defence were to be put into action against Britain, and sixty-four newly equipped German divisions would be in the field.

The Reich would continue to do all it could to help its Italian ally, but the extent of the help asked for was grossly excessive. The request for the transfer to Italy of 2,000 aircraft was out of the question. A matter for strong criticism was the shortage of properly equipped air fields in Italy. Rigorous action must be taken in this respect, and in expropriating private property regard for private interests must be swept aside. Rigorous action must also be taken to improve the discipline of the Italian troops. As in Germany, courts-martial must act energetically and make use of the death penalty. The struggle for victory of the Fascist and Nazi revolutions must not be left to be completed by the next generation.[24]

The present-day reader, free from the pressures of the time, noting the references in the report of the interpreter Dr. Paul Schmidt to the technical improvements and prospects of increased German military strength announced by Hitler at Feltre, might be tempted to conclude that there was justification for regarding the military outlook of the Axis as being favourable in some respects.

But anyone familiar with the Italian background, and in particular the total lack of resources and the general war-weariness, could, in view of the allied penetration into the country that grew deeper daily, regard Hitler's optimistic flood of eloquence only as

[24] A.A. Pol. Arch., Büro Reichsminister, Handakten Dolmetscher Schmidt, 1943, Part II, Nos. 49255–99.

a dance of will-o'-the-wisps. At all events, it contained no concrete promise of immediate aid.

Ambrosio and his suite were dumbfounded when the conversation with Hitler ended without Mussolini having contributed anything except a few insignificant interpolations. The Italian dictator did not feel well that day, and was obviously in continual pain.

Also he was upset by something that happened while the conversations were in progress. After Hitler had been speaking for about an hour, his private secretary, De Cesare, handed him a note informing him that Rome had just been raided by a strong force of allied bombers. Rome had not previously been bombed.

Mussolini did not conceal how greatly he was disturbed by this piece of news; he passed the note to Hitler in a state of extreme agitation. It was characteristic of Hitler that he did not devote a single word to it. Mussolini presumably expected him to express regret at what might have been the beginning of the possible destruction of Rome, but Hitler behaved as if he were deaf and unconcernedly continued his harangue on the future conduct of the war.

According to Colonel Montezemolo, Mussolini subsequently expressed to his entourage his obviously genuine regret at not having been in Rome that day.

After the end of his conference with Hitler, Mussolini had to listen on the same afternoon to the stormy remonstrances of his suite at his failure to keep his word and discuss Italy's future with Hitler. Colonel-General Ambrosio displayed his indignation openly. He pointed out the consequences of the rejection of the request for immediate German arms deliveries, and actually called on Mussolini to end the war within a fortnight.[25]

Mussolini said he would discuss the matter with Hitler on the way to the airfield, but again failed to do so. In Rome on 20 July, when Ambrosio again remonstrated with him about his silence, he replied that he would write to Hitler that Italy must withdraw from the war.

He did not do that either. From the historical point of view it is important that during those days Mussolini himself several times mentioned the idea of withdrawing from the war, though in his confusion and indecision he could not make up his mind.

[25] Giuseppe Bastianini, *Uomini, Cose, Fatti*, Vitagliano, 1959, p. 120 f.

Colonel-General Ambrosio had separate conversations with Field-Marshal Keitel at Feltre, and it made a great impression on him that the Chief of the German High Command still spoke with confidence of the defensive successes to be expected in Sicily, but at the same time emphasized that German reinforcements could be sent only after a considerable delay. Ambrosio saw a disastrous anomaly between this attitude and the rapid Anglo-American advance and the crumbling of German–Italian resistance in Sicily, and henceforward regarded the Italian military situation as beyond repair.

On 21 July Alessandro Melchiori told me about a conversation he had had with Mussolini about the Feltre meeting. At Klessheim in April Hitler had succeeded in temporarily restoring some of Mussolini's confidence, but at Feltre he failed to repeat the performance. Nevertheless Hitler was convinced that he had once more 'brought Mussolini completely into line'.[26] Mussolini was finally disillusioned with Hitler's appreciations of the situation, which had been consistently over-optimistic since the end of 1940; Melchiori said that he now shared the Comando Supremo view of the insufficiency of German aid. The only interesting thing that Hitler had said had been about the development of secret weapons, but Italy's fate hung in the balance, and the miracle weapons would be too late. Melchiori added that Mussolini was no longer the same man.

Since the allied landing in Sicily and the conversation with Hitler at Feltre he had changed. Melchiori described his new condition as semi-apathy, and he attributed this more to his downcast mood than to the deterioration in his health. He still displayed his quick grasp of essentials, but he no longer had the energy to make quick decisions and give clear and unambiguous orders. He let things take their course, and at times actually created the impression of being a tired onlooker who inwardly mocked the zeal of others. The only thing capable of shaking him out of his lethargy would be German divisions in large numbers.

A detail Melchiori also mentioned was that Mussolini feared that the population would resent his absence from Rome during the first air raid on the Italian capital. This raid had affected him deeply; he regarded it as a bad omen for the future.

The British had raided Rome on 19 July for the purpose of

[26] Warlimont, p. 354 f.

destroying railway installations. The British Air Marshal Tedder himself took part in the raid for the purpose of personally ensuring that dwellings and artistic monuments were spared. Nevertheless a broad bombing carpet was laid on the San Lorenzo quarter, where an especially poverty-stricken section of the population lived. That this was done in error was shown by the fact that the bombs were dropped in a curve parallel to a stretch of railway track farther out from the centre of the city. The excitement in a city that had hitherto been spared the direct impact of war was very great. Those who could took their cars, unregistered because of wartime conditions, from garages or sheds, carefully filled the tank with petrol hoarded in the cellar for emergencies, and made off. On the evening of 19 July the police indulgently watched this variegated exodus by way of all the exits from the city of prohibited and often no longer very safe vehicles.

There was further excitement on the night of 20–21 July, though its cause and its originators were never discovered. At about 11 p.m. the Via Nomentana and all the neighbouring streets and squares near my flat were filled with anxious people who began fleeing in the direction of the city centre, taking prams and light luggage with them. Soon afterwards an excited young policeman appeared at our house, telling everyone who lived in it to leave immediately, taking immediate necessities with them. He said that dangerous explosions were going to take place. I did not follow these instructions.

People were to be seen thronging towards the city centre until the early hours of the morning. It later turned out that a large proportion of the inhabitants of Rome had taken part in a night march, often of many hours' duration, to seek shelter in the city centre. They returned to their homes in the course of the day, exhausted and upset. Either a mere rumour had started this panic by an already nervous population, or a group of agitators had artificially fomented it for political reasons.

On 23 July General von Rintelen devoted a full teleprinted report to Italian reactions to the Feltre meeting.[27] The most important points were as follows. The Comando Supremo was gravely concerned that aid could not be provided in the form of a far greater number of German troops. It had always been assumed

[27] MGFA DZ, Akte W o 1–7/286, Fernschreiben des Militär-Attaché Rom, 1a No. 2678/43, Geheime Kommandosache.

D

that when a second front was opened in the Mediterranean strong German reserves, particularly armoured formations, would be sent immediately. The mood of the population remained depressed, as it had been before. It no longer believed that there was the slightest chance of victory, and rejected all attempts to influence it through its own press and radio. Things had got to such a pitch that now its only hope was in the later magnanimity of the enemy.

Rintelen knew very well how little Hitler and his entourage appreciated such frankness. He had already once been ordered to headquarters in the autumn of 1940 and sharply reprimanded for having anticipated in his reports the severe Italian set-backs in North Africa and Greece that subsequently took place. He nevertheless continued to regard it as the supreme duty of a military attaché to record his impressions and views in his reports without regard to the sensitivities of the recipients.

On 20 July Mussolini had secretly summoned the members of the Grand Council of the Fascist Party to attend a meeting at the Palazzo Venezia at 5 p.m. on 24 July. The German Ambassador discovered from the garrulous Roberto Farinacci on Wednesday, 21 July, that the Grand Council was going to meet 'at the end of the week', but Farinacci did not mention the date. Farinacci had always favoured the greatest Italian dependence on Germany; he actually told Germans in confidential conversations that in his opinion the whole Italian army should be put under German command. He left Mackensen with the impression that he and his friends were going to argue in the Grand Council for a more streamlined conduct of the war, on the German model. This alleviated any anxieties Mackensen may have felt that the meeting might lead to unpleasant surprises. As a result of his passing on this gossip of Farinacci's, the German leadership was given a reassuring but totally false picture of the situation.[28] This was yet another instance of the ambassador's preferring one-sided information. In this instance, however, the situation was confused by the further piece of information that Mussolini had recently been in close consultation with Dino Grandi, the former Minister of Justice and one-time Italian Ambassador in London. Grandi had for a long time been known to be increasingly dissociating himself from the Fascist government. In view of his strong personality, he could be expected to attack, not just government policy, but the wavering

[28] Goebbels, p. 367; Kirkpatrick, p. 518.

authoritarian régime itself. On the other hand, Mussolini on 22 July described him to a German visitor as a loyal follower.[29]

The three days that passed after the forthcoming meeting of the Grand Council became known were marked by ever-increasing uncertainty. Apart from some confused hints by Farinacci, a secrecy unusual in Italy was maintained by the participants about the resolutions that were to be proposed. Neither the leading figures in the party, who were divided among themselves, nor diplomatic observers nor public opinion at large dared forecast what would happen. Even those most knowledgeable about the Roman scene, both before and behind the footlights, did not know whether Fascism's hour of crisis had come. Even the members of the Grand Council had no idea where the ball they had set in motion would roll.

At midday on 24 July General Rintelen reported by teleprinter to the German High Command and the Army General Staff, attachés' department, as follows:

1. Since the conversations at Feltre doubt has prevailed in all authoritative military and political circles whether Germany will be in a position to give Italy sufficient aid against the invasion.

2. The Fascist Grand Council is meeting on 24 July. Great significance is to be attributed to this meeting in the circumstances. It is said that a group in the Grand Council will call for stronger and more energetic government. It is also said that the Duce will be made to surrender his personal leadership of the three defence ministries.[30]

[29] Kesselring, p. 229 f.
[30] MGFA DZ, Akte W o 1–7/286, Militär-Attaché Rom, 1a No. 2694/43 Geheime Kommandosache.

II

Dictator's Downfall

July 1943 was unusually hot in central Italy. The notorious scirocco, which normally reaches its height in the following months, arrived several weeks earlier and was more violent than usual in the *conca di Roma*, the Rome basin. The temperature did not drop even at night.

Outwardly 24 July passed quietly. The population had not yet fully appreciated the implications of the summoning of the Fascist Grand Council for that afternoon. By late evening the only news was that it was still in session. The Palazzo Venezia was heavily guarded and cordoned off.

Next day, Sunday, 25 July, the news was that discussions had gone on vigorously until 3 a.m., but with no positive results; it was said that Mussolini wanted time to consider his attitude to the various resolutions on the agenda. We were told that he had now returned to his desk at the Palazzo Venezia, that he was going to receive the newly appointed Japanese Ambassador at midday, and that it was expected that he would then be received in audience by King Victor Emmanuel III so that he might inform the latter about the meeting of the Grand Council. Only Counsellor Mollier, the head of the Embassy press department, was given a vague hint that Mussolini's position had been shaken.

General von Rintelen, fulfilling a long-standing engagement, spent the day with a German division north of Rome. Field-Marshal Kesselring was also absent from his headquarters at Frascati during the hours of daylight.

Shortly after 8 p.m. I received a telephone call at my flat from Field-Marshal Kesselring's staff, asking me to get in touch with the Comando Supremo to arrange for the Field-Marshal to see Mussolini as quickly as possible in connection with an urgent military matter. It had not been possible to make any contact with Mussolini from the German headquarters at Frascati. I telephoned the Comando Supremo and talked to my friend Major Marchesi, who was on Ambrosio's staff. He told me that the request could not be

complied with, and asked me not to press him further, because I should be getting more news soon. Also he hoped to be able to make me some interesting revelations next day. I asked him provocatively whether Signor Mussolini had gone away by any chance. He laughed, and said: 'No, but perhaps he is still with the King.'

At 10.45 p.m. loud shouts and cries of jubilation in the street echoed through the open window: *Viva l'Italia! Viva il Re! Viva Badoglio!* I switched on the radio. The proclamation by the King and Marshal Pietro Badoglio was just coming through. Apart from the news that the King had accepted Mussolini's resignation, assumed supreme command of the armed forces, and appointed Badoglio chief of government, the most striking thing about it were the words *la guerra continua* ('the war goes on'). Our cook burst into the room, dancing with joy, and exclaimed: *Lo ammazzeranno finalmente* ('they'll end by killing him', meaning Mussolini), just when I was trying to put through a top priority call to the German High Command. General von Rintelen had not yet returned to Rome. The exchange at the German High Command refused to connect me; all communications with Italy had been ordered to be cut. The officer in charge of the telephone service and the officer in charge of communications, to whom I tried to explain what was happening, said that there were strict orders that made it impossible for them to comply with my request, even when I asked to be put through to General Jodl or Field-Marshal Keitel.

At 11.15 p.m. I was again telephoned by the staff of the Supreme Commander South, asking me to arrange with the Comando Supremo for Field-Marshal Kesselring to be received by the King that same night. This request was again politely but firmly declined by the Italians.[1]

Many Romans remained in the streets that night to celebrate the occasion. Crowds gathered outside the Quirinal, the royal palace, to express their pleasure and loyalty. They did not know that the King had not left his town residence, the Villa Savoia.

At about midnight I received an appeal for help from the staff of the German House in Rome. I was told that the crowd that had gathered in the Piazza di Spagna was trying to set fire to the place, which had once been an artists' home and then became a meeting-place for the Nazi Party in Rome. I immediately telephoned

[1] Kesselring, p. 231.

Ambrosio's deputy, General Francesco Rossi, at the Comando Supremo, who promised that appropriate measures would be taken immediately. Shortly afterwards Major Marchesi telephoned on General Rossi's behalf to say that there must have been a misunderstanding. Only rejoicings were taking place in the Piazza di Spagna, and they had nothing to do with the German House. Half an hour before he, Marchesi, had seen a German car held up in the centre of the city and the occupants enthusiastically greeted with cries of *Viva Germania e viva l'Italia!*

Next morning, 26 July, the drive to the office was very wearisome and time-wasting. Again and again I had to make detours because of processions. Long columns of all age-groups, waving green, white, and red flags, blocked the streets. Some held aloft pictures of the King, and soon there were pictures of Badoglio too. Flags flew everywhere, and decorated pictures of the royal couple and the new head of the government appeared in shop windows. There were bonfires of Fascist uniforms, offices of party newspapers were demolished, and everywhere Fascist emblems were trampled underfoot. A car went down the Via Nazionale dragging a bust of Mussolini on a chain behind it, and boys battered it with sticks to the accompaniment of shouts of joy. A tram bore the legend *È finito il carnevale tragico* ('The tragic carnival is over'). Particularly striking were transparents with the text: 'We want to go to the front, we want to fight for the King and Badoglio, but not for Fascism.'[2]

At the Embassy, naturally enough, the atmosphere was tense. Nobody could sit quietly at his desk, and lively discussions ensued. Doertenbach told me how the first contact with the Badoglio government had been established. On the previous evening the Duke of Acquarone, the Minister of the Royal Household, had telephoned the Embassy to transmit Badoglio's request that the ambassador should call on him immediately. The answer given on Mackensen's instructions was that he was not available. Half an hour later an officer appeared at the ambassador's residence to repeat the request, but the ambassador declined to receive him. The officer thereupon asked that a representative of the ambassador might be sent to Badoglio, and Mackensen deputed Doertenbach for the purpose. Doertenbach asked for instructions in

[2] MGFA DZ, Akte W o 1–7/286, Militär-Attaché Rom, 1a No. 2703/43, Geheime Kommandosache, 26.7.1943.

writing, and Mackensen jotted down on a piece of paper: 'Go and see Badoglio, but be careful, Badoglio is not on the right side.' Doertenbach showed me this note.

After returning from his interview with the new head of the Italian government, he told me that the latter had said that he regretted having had to receive the Japanese Ambassador before seeing a representative of the Reich government, because the German Ambassador had not reacted to his invitation to call on him immediately. He then went on to say that the change of government brought about by the King implied no change in the conduct of the war or in Italian foreign policy. He asked that his good wishes might be sent to the German head of state.

To judge the behaviour of the King and the Badoglio government, we must briefly retrace our steps and describe the course and outcome of the meeting of the Fascist Grand Council.

Mussolini had been forced to call the 24 July meeting by the highest ranking Fascists and members of the council. The grave military defeats, the deterioration in the Duce's health, and his being overburdened with political leadership and simultaneous supreme command of the armed forces made a reorganization, if not more, essential in their view. But there were sharp differences of opinion among the members of the council, who numbered twenty-eight (excluding Mussolini), about exactly what should be done. It is certain that nearly all of them wanted to persuade Mussolini to give up the supreme command and hand it back to the King. Most of them, in harmony with the general feeling of the people, looked to the monarchy, exercising a new and real authority, to hold the disintegrating nation together. The pillar represented by the party had grown rickety, so the pillar of the monarchy must be strengthened to save the state structure from collapse. That this was playing with fire so far as the Fascist régime was concerned was accepted by members of the Grand Council in different ways.

The chief issue at the meeting was Grandi's resolution,[3] which said:

The Grand Council of Fascism, meeting in this supreme hour of trial, thinks in the first place of the heroic warriors of all arms who are renewing the noble traditions of valour and inexhaustible self-sacrifice of our

[3] Grandi, p. 41.

glorious armed forces, side by side with the proud population of Sicily, in whose attitude the loyalty of the Italian people find a brilliant example.

Having examined the internal and external situation and the political and military conducts of the war,

it declares that it is the sacred duty of all Italians at all costs to defend the unity, independence, and freedom of the country, the fruit of the sacrifices and efforts of four generations since its rebirth, the life and future of the Italian people,

confirms the necessity of the moral and material unity of all Italians in this hard hour of decision for the nation's fate,

declares that for this purpose the immediate re-establishment of all state functions is necessary by restoring to the Crown, the Grand Council, the Government, Parliament, and the Corporations the duties promised them under the basic laws,

invites the chief of government to ask his Majesty the King, to whom the heart of the whole nation turns in loyalty and confidence, for the sake of the honour and salvation of the country to assume, by taking command of the armed forces by land, sea, and air in accordance with Article V of the Constitution of the Kingdom, that supreme initiative of decision that our institutions place upon him and that always in the whole of our national history has been the glorious heritage of our noble dynasty of Savoy.

It has since become generally known that Grandi's purpose in framing this resolution was to bring about Mussolini's fall. Its acceptance by the Grand Council was intended to provide the King with legal means of bringing about a change of government. After his talk with the King on 3 June Grandi believed he was justified in assuming that in such circumstances the King would take this step. The King, however, had avoided committing himself.

A number of Grandi's colleagues, headed by Federzoni, backed the resolution with more or less the same purpose in mind, while others wanted to use it merely to secure a substantial reduction in Mussolini's responsibilities and burden of work. In their view, the King should assume the command of the armed forces, while the responsibility and freedom of action of Ministers should be increased, and generals in key positions should be relieved of their command if they could be shown to have been responsible for failures by the Italian armies. Some of the backers of the resolution were willing to take account of the party's weakness to the extent of agreeing that ministerial posts might be open in the future to

personalities who were not members of the party if there were sound reasons to justify their appointment.

In the short time available before the meeting, this variety of aims made it difficult for Grandi to obtain enough signatures for his resolution. That also explains why he framed it in such general terms without more plainly expressing his own much more far-reaching objectives. The members of the Grand Council were divided. They were torn between seeing that something must be done and the fear that, if Mussolini succeeded in surviving the crisis, he might later hold them to account.

Farinacci tabled another resolution. This also included an appeal to the King, but called for a strengthening of the party and a declaration of loyalty to the German ally. But Farinacci had long since lost his credibility, and his position in the party was now so shaken that he had practically no support. Also everyone knew that he expected the crisis to lead to still greater Italian subjection to German leadership and hoped for a high position for himself as a result.

A third resolution, tabled by Scorza, the party secretary, had no influence on the course of the meeting.

Mussolini began by speaking for two hours. He tried to divert attention from the acuteness of the Italian military plight by talking about secondary matters and enumerating mistakes that had been made in the North African campaign, particularly by Rommel. He did not mention the meagre results of the Feltre meeting, but spoke highly of German aid, specifying the total deliveries that had been received from Germany since the Italian intervention in the war. He devoted the main part of his speech to replying to Grandi's resolution, which he rightly regarded as an attack on his authority. All the members of the Grand Council spoke in the long discussion that followed, and the Duce was called on, now sharply, now appeasingly, to relieve himself of his burdens. One of the few who supported him was Galbiati, the chief of the militia. Alfieri, the Italian Ambassador in Berlin, repeated his warnings that Germany would send no more real aid and that Hitler regarded the fighting in Italy only as a battle to gain time before the battle for his own country began. Even Scorza called for reforms and new methods, though without calling for restoration of supreme authority to the King.

The vote at the end of the meeting resulted in nineteen votes for Grandi's resolution, seven against, and one abstention. Farinacci

was the only one to vote for his own resolution. Stories that the proceedings resembled a Wild West film, that blows were exchanged and that some of those present fainted, are incorrect. It is correct, however, that most of those who attended took pistols with them as a precaution.

Mussolini behaved moderately throughout the meeting, and only seldom in his hour of crisis did he answer sharply. He seemed to content himself with playing down the dangers of the situation and the seriousness of the resolutions. He referred to new plans for the more efficient conduct of the war, and above all tried to be conciliatory. No doubt he hoped once more to be able to pacify the King and survive the crisis by playing for time. He rejected secret suggestions by the last of his loyal followers that he should have Grandi and other opponents arrested out of hand. He knew that at this stage he could no longer hope to extricate himself from this predicament by violent measures.

The Grand Council broke up without knowing what would happen next. All eyes were on the King, to whom Mussolini would now have to report.

While events were leading up to this dramatic climax in government and party, Victor Emmanuel III, who was seventy-three, had been preparing to face yet another of the vital historical decisions of his long reign—he had mounted the throne in 1900 in succession to his assassinated father Umberto I. He knew what the nation expected of him. The number of those who tried to express their anxieties and hopes to him had steadily increased. The Duke of Acquarone, the Minister of the Royal Household, had arranged meetings between him and numerous critical and experienced personalities, so that nothing of the full tragedy of the Italian situation should remain concealed from him. Among those who tried to influence him against Mussolini, the most prominent had been first Bonomi and finally Ambrosio. Bonomi, who had been Prime Minister in 1921 and 1922 and had advised him in 1922, the tense year of the March on Rome, had recommended him to take radical steps at the beginning of June. He had proposed not only that Mussolini should be dismissed, but that Italy should dissociate herself from Germany immediately. The discredited Fascist régime, he said, had no more right to involve Italy in its downfall than the dead had to drag the living down to the grave.[4]

[4] Bonomi, p. 41 f.

In his capacity as Chief of the Comando Supremo it was Ambrosio's duty to report to the King on the military situation only at long intervals. He did this without embroidering anything. But eventually he grew bolder, and confessed to the King that in view of the situation he felt it his duty at the Comando Supremo to make preparations for the eventuality of a change of government. A conversation on this matter took place at Ambrosio's request on 6 July.[5] Ambrosio's attitude shows that he had no thought of taking any action without orders from the head of state.

To Bonomi and Ambrosio and all the others whom he received the King maintained the same outward reserve. Bonomi says that he betrayed his thoughts by no word or gesture. He merely expressed his thanks for his visitors' excellent intentions and complained about the unsatisfactory state of his health.[6]

He did not want to be precipitate. Above all, he was determined not to intervene while there was the slightest chance of Mussolini's bringing about an end of the war in a way that would be tolerable to Italy. He knew of course from the regular bi-weekly audiences he gave Mussolini that the latter had several times had in mind approaching Hitler in this respect, for instance with the proposal that Germany should end the war in Russia.

Thus all the King's visitors who wanted drastic royal intervention left without receiving a clear answer. But the mere fact that he listened to them led them to conclude that he would not fail them when the hour came. Above all, the cool, calculating, reserved monarch waited for a constitutional handle to be put within his reach; he wanted a constitutional way out, not a *coup d'état*. Forced as he was to maintain the greatest secrecy, and in an incalculable war situation that changed almost from day to day, he could make plans only in broad outline and for the short term.

Subsequent reconstruction of events shows that until the meeting of the Grand Council the King and his few advisers wanted to dismiss the Duce and set up a military government. It was clear to the King that in that event Mussolini must immediately be put under arrest. The possibility of Fascist reactions had to be taken into account, and Mussolini must therefore vanish from the political scene. His arrest also seemed necessary for his own protection.

The King had also decided that the new administration must be

[5] Puntoni, p. 136 f.   [6] Bonomi, p. 7.

a military government with expert ministers. He believed that this was the best way to meet the war situation. With a stubbornness that was characteristic of him he rejected suggestions by his advisers that a political cabinet should be formed.

Since the beginning of July he had also been considering the question of whom he should call on to head the new government. He hesitated between the two veteran marshals Caviglia and Badoglio. The even older Admiral Thaon De Revel was also considered as a possibility. The King had a conversation with Badoglio on 15 July. The King wished only to assure himself that he could count on the Marshal, and no decision was made. General von Rintelen knew from many years' official and personal contact with Badoglio that relations between him and the King were not unclouded. It was known that after the Marshals' return from the Abyssinian war, which ended in victory for Italy, the King had not presented him with his autographed picture, and the omission of this usual gesture had upset him. Also General Paolo Puntoni, who had been aide-de-camp to the King since 1939, confirms in his diary that the King had personal reservations about Badoglio, though he recognized his great reputation among the Italian people.[7]

Those who can put themselves back into the tense situation of those days and weeks will understand that it was impossible for the King and his advisers to make plans looking beyond Mussolini's dismissal and the setting up of a military government. The overriding question was, of course, how crippled Italy could continue the war. Relations with Nazi Germany had to be taken into account in connection with everything. No opponent of the Fascist régime could for the time being do more than concentrate his efforts on reducing the hopeless disorder that prevailed in the country. The chief consideration was to do so with the minimum of harm to it, and this took precedence over everything. No one could foresee what the next day would bring. In regard to what lay farther ahead, those who wanted a change of government could nourish no more than conjectures and hopes; there is plenty of evidence that that was indeed the situation. Both the hectic, agitated atmosphere that prevailed and the occasional resurgences of Mussolini while he remained in office accorded with an urgent desire to end the war as quickly as possible.

[7] Puntoni, p. 136 f.

Meanwhile the King was very well aware that ending the war did not depend on Italy alone, but also on the allies and Germany. Thus Deakin's careful investigation of his plans[8] has produced no evidence that he succumbed to the temptation of associating the idea of a change of government with concrete ideas for extricating Italy from the war. He was too intelligent to reckon without the hosts, i.e. the allies and Germany. For the further development of Italian politics their attitude to the new post-Fascist Italy must be awaited.

He decided to act after Colonel-General Ambrosio informed him of the outcome of the Feltre conversations on 19 July. He considered the time was now overripe for taking the country's destiny into his hands. The leading Fascists' revolt against Mussolini provided the final demonstration that the head of the government was no longer fit for his task.

The meeting of the Grand Council gave him the right and the duty to carry out the will of the vast majority of the population. Grandi informed the Duke of Acquarone of the course and outcome of the meeting at 4 a.m. on 25 July.[9] He suggested that Marshal Caviglia should head the new government, but Acquarone replied that the King inclined towards Badoglio.[10] This shows the extent to which the upheaval of 25 July developed out of the situation and how little it was planned.

Marshal Badoglio was informed by the Duke of Acquarone only at the last moment that the King had finally decided to appoint him chief of government in Mussolini's place.

Our press officer, Professor Herbert Gericke, who was a major in the reserve, and his wife had for a long time been on terms of friendship with the Badoglio family. Gericke found out that on the afternoon of 25 July Badoglio had been playing bridge at his home and said in the course of the game that he would give a great deal to know what had happened overnight at the meeting of the Grand Council. His ignorance about what was going on accorded with the confusion of the situation. At this time Mussolini was being received in audience by the King at the Villa Savoia. This time the Duce's attempt to belittle the situation made no impression. When he left the villa he was arrested. The arrangements for this had been hurriedly improvised, but they were sufficient, because secrecy was maintained. Not a finger was lifted in his defence, and he had no alternative but to resign.

[8] Deakin, pp. 340 and 423.   [9] Grandi, p. 57.   [10] Deakin, p. 467.

Badoglio in the saddle

All the news that reached the German Embassy on 26 July, and all the personal impressions of the Embassy staff, confirmed that Fascism had collapsed like a house of cards and had thus ceased to exist as a viable régime for Italy. Even those who for years had been aware of the régime's weakness and the people's dislike of it were impressed by the fact that such an overwhelming majority approved of the change. At all events, a convincing vote had been given for the King and the Badoglio government, and it was impossible to doubt the legality of that government.

Hitler, however, completely mistook the new situation in Italy from the outset, or simply refused to believe it. At a conference at his headquarters on the afternoon of 26 July he delivered himself of the view that 'the new régime of course has no one behind it but the Jews and rabble who are making themselves conspicuous in Rome'. He also spoke of 'Fascist steel' and of the intention very quickly to build-up 'many things' again.[11] His preconceived ideas necessarily constituted a very dangerous stumbling-block in the way of future German–Italian co-operation.

The first test for the new Italian government was provided by Communist unrest in Upper Italy. Badoglio had it suppressed.

A state of siege was declared in Rome at 1 p.m. on 26 July. General Rossi informed General von Rintelen that this was a precautionary measure, expected to be of brief duration. The general pleasure at the sudden upheaval had caused people to leave their work and flock into the streets. They had at first deliberately been given the opportunity 'to walk their legs off', but now order must be restored.

Meetings of more than three persons were forbidden, and a total curfew was imposed from 9 p.m. Restaurants, theatres, and cinemas were shut. The Piave Division moved into Rome and occupied key points. The German Embassy received special permission to use the streets at night.

Ambassador von Mackensen was received by Badoglio in his improvised office in the Italian Ministry of the Interior at 10 a.m. on 26 July, and Field-Marshal Kesselring and General von Rintelen were received by him during the afternoon. Badoglio reiterated the assurances that had been given to Doertenbach on the

---

[11] Lage, Vol. 10, pp. 369 and 373.

previous evening, namely that the change of government involved no change in Italian policy. A more stream-lined organization of all Italian forces would ensue.

Mackensen added to the report of his conversation some illuminating details about certain external circumstances. He had driven to the Ministry of the Interior in an open car, wearing diplomatic uniform. Some uncomplimentary remarks had been shouted at him, but there had also been manifestations of friendliness to Germany. The whole picture showed the aimlessness of the mass of the population.[12]

Badoglio informed his German visitors of an exchange of letters with Mussolini. On the evening of 25 July he had written to the former dictator, informing him that measures had had to be taken to ensure his safety and asking him where he wished to reside. On the same evening Mussolini had replied as follows from his place of arrest:

1. I feel obliged to thank Marshal Badoglio for his concern for my person.

2. The only place I have at my disposal for my future residence is La Rocca delle Caminate. I am ready to go there at any time.

3. I assure Marshal Badoglio, recalling our work together in past times, that for my part, not only shall I put no difficulties in his way, but am ready to co-operate with him in any way.

4. I welcome the decision that has been made to continue the war by the side of our ally, as is required by the interests and honour of the country at this time. I hope that the Marshal's heavy task, which he has undertaken by order and in the name of his Majesty the King, whose loyal servant I was for twenty years and still am, will be crowned by success. Long live Italy!

Benito Mussolini.[13]

It is impossible to withhold respect for Mussolini for the attitude expressed in this letter. It would be unfair to regard it merely as the outcome of anxiety about his future felt by a man who had just been put under arrest. With this letter he abdicated. Even though it could be regarded as merely another sample of the heady nationalist rhetoric then current both in Italy and Germany, in his darkest hour he nevertheless showed himself to be a patriot.

Above all, the letter throws light on the arbitrariness of Hitler's

---

[12] A.A. Pol. Arch., Italien, Vol. 14, Nos, 72455–7.
[13] Vanna Vailati, *Badoglio risponde*, Milan, 1960, p. 90.

action eight weeks later, when he had Mussolini abducted from his place of imprisonment and made him head of the artificial Fascist rump republic in northern Italy.

The letter also illustrates the glaring difference in the mentality of the two dictators. While Mussolini on the day of his downfall wished his successor and his country well, we know that in April 1945 Hitler declared that Germany had not shown herself worthy of winning the war under his leadership and therefore deserved no better fate than to go down with him. He had already made a statement to similar effect in a speech to national leaders and Gauleiters on 3 August 1944.[14]

This exchange of letters also shows that the King and Badoglio intended after a brief transitional period to transfer Mussolini from his secret place of arrest to a self-chosen place of residence where he would be merely kept under guard.[15] But, as the Germans started tirelessly searching for him, and the Italians soon discovered that Hitler was proposing to 'get him out' by force, this plan had to be dropped.

Farinacci had already taken refuge in the German Embassy on the night of 24–5 July, and on the 26th the news spread in the Embassy that he had been sent to Germany at his own request. In fact Mackensen, with Kesselring's help, had had him sent to Munich by special aircraft, wearing Luftwaffe uniform. Mussolini's son Vittorio was sent to Germany in the same way, and on 28 July Preziosi followed, also in a special aircraft and in German uniform.[16]

This calls for two comments. In the first place, it was surprising that more pro-German Fascists did not follow suit, either for fear of reprisals or to put themselves at the German disposal against Badoglio. This showed the impact made by the statements by the King and Badoglio that nobody would be called to account on political grounds; it also showed that these Italians realized that Fascism had had its day. Ribbentrop, far from appreciating this, sent a telegram on 26 July asking that more pro-German Fascists should be sent to Germany in German uniform to support countermeasures against the Badoglio government. He inquired in

[14] Max Domarus, *Hitler: Reden und Proklamationen*, Vol. II, Würzburg, 1963, p. 2139. Percy Ernst Schramm, *Das Ende des Krieges*, Cologne and Opladen, 1965, p. 48 f.

[15] Kirkpatrick, p. 540.

[16] A.A. Pol. Arch., Italien, Vol. 14, No. 72518.

particular about Scorza and Bastianini.[17] But Bastianini was not to be found. Scorza maintained cautious contact with the Embassy from his hiding-place, because Mackensen appealed to him to fall in with this 'invitation'.

Secondly, this behaviour by the Ambassador, Field-Marshal Kesselring and the German Foreign Minister violated the rules of international law.

International law recognizes the right of a state to grant asylum to foreigners who take refuge in its territory for political reasons only on certain conditions. It recognizes no such thing as a diplomatic right of asylum. Embassies and ministries are on principle not entitled to accept political refugees. Thus, if an embassy of a foreign country gives refuge to such a fugitive and then sends him secretly to that country, and in foreign uniform into the bargain, a very substantial breach of international rules has been committed.

When actions that are dubious under the rules of international law have been committed, attempts are often made to explain and justify them by appealing to unusual circumstances. Thus in this case it was subsequently argued that these Fascists were needed by Hitler in defence of legitimate German interests. It was also claimed that there was justification for the first impression that the Badoglio government had been established against the people's will and would very soon be overthrown, and hence that it was a duty to support the opponents of that government in every way. The baselessness of this excuse was demonstrated by events, and the appeal to exceptional circumstances can therefore not be maintained.

Farinacci and Preziosi were a great disappointment to Hitler, Ribbentrop, and Goebbels. At their very first conversations at German headquarters they criticized Mussolini. According to Goebbels, they showed themselves to be selfish muddleheads, unusable for the counter-measures intended,[18] and for that reason alone Mackensen should have avoided this legally dubious action. Dollmann, who enthusiastically supported it, in fact did no service to his master Himmler in the matter.

A few days later Mackensen himself displayed doubts both about the utility and legality of the action. When yet another Fascist, Alessandro Pavolini, applied to be smuggled to Germany, he tele-

---

[17] Ibid., No. 72495.   [18] Goebbels, pp. 378 and 382.

graphed to Berlin on 31 July inquiring whether 'the risk of illegal evacuation in the face of the new government should again be undertaken'.[19]

On the afternoon of 26 July news arrived that fifty or sixty youths had forced their way into the German consulate-general at Turin, thrown furniture and documents into the street, and assaulted von Langen, the Consul-General. Reports from consulates and German military units everywhere else in Italy, however, coincided with our own observations of the Italian attitude. The people were delighted at the overthrow of Fascism and, while some were rather reserved in their attitude to the Germans, generally their behaviour was very correct, and sometimes actually noticeably friendlier than before.

As a result of the raid on the consulate-general at Turin, Ambassador von Mackensen was instructed to protest sharply to Badoglio, which he did on 28 July. The Marshal replied that this deplorable incident had obviously been the work of a deluded, isolated group. The government naturally accepted responsibility and would take sharp measures. In response to this justified German protest Badoglio went as far as to give orders on the same day that the offenders should be tried by a military court and that the Prefect of Turin should be relieved of his office.[20]

These measures were duly carried out. The dismissal of a prefect who was totally guiltless in the matter went so far beyond the reactions normal in such circumstances that it roused the suspicion that the new government had in any case wanted to get rid of this representative of the old Fascist hierarchy. This could not be proved, however, and the drastic measures by which Badoglio responded to the German protest could be regarded only as a sign of good will and a determination to avoid disturbing German–Italian co-operation.

I went to the Comando Supremo in the early afternoon of 26 July. In the corridor I first ran into General Castellano, who became well known later because he conducted the armistice negotiations with the allies and signed the armistice for Italy on 3 September 1943 at Cassibile in Sicily. I had several times met this short, sharp-witted Sicilian in conversations on military and political matters arising out of the operations in Africa. At a German–Italian conference that lasted for several days in March 1942 we

[19] A.A. Pol. Arch., Italien, Vol. 14, No. 72671.   [20] Ibid., No. 72580.

had long conversations in the evening about the conduct of the war and German–Italian relations.

Even then it was easy to see that he was no supporter of linking the fate of the two countries on Nazi–Fascist lines and regarded the war prospects as gloomy in the extreme. This time he was in a great hurry, and greeted me briefly with a significant remark: 'How nice of you to come and congratulate us straight away. *Adesso stiamo meglio* (now we feel better).'

Then, as usual, without having been announced, I knocked at the door of the head of the operations section, Colonel Giuseppe Cordero Lanza di Montezemolo. Colonel Nurra, however, was sitting in his chair. I had known Colonel Nurra for the past fortnight. He was now taking over Montezemolo's duties, because Montezemolo had been designated to another appointment and had left the busy and responsible post he had held for several years.

Nurra, looking gaunt and rather bent, but with his usual extremely friendly expression, rose from behind his big yellow desk in the big, bright room of the Palazzo Vidoni and broke the news straight away. 'You will not be seeing our common friend Montezemolo here again,' he said. 'He was appointed Badoglio's *chef de cabinet* this morning. The Marshal wanted to emphasize that in war-time military matters take precedence over everything else. We are delighted that first-class liaison has thus been established between the head of the government and the Comando Supremo.'

Nurra immediately had me put through to the Ministry of the Interior, so that I could offer Montezemolo my congratulations. With his usual courtesy, he apologized for not having been able to get into contact with me since his appointment, but the first measures being taken by the new government had kept him more than fully occupied. As the change of government had taken place overnight, without the slightest preparation, he was now having to make the most primitive arrangements for the work of his office. True, there had been no difficulty in requisitioning pencils and paper at the Ministry of the Interior, but he was now working against time choosing the necessary staff. He said that, so far from seeing less of each other in future, the unusual circumstances would cause our contact to be closer. We should see each other daily or, if that was impossible, telephone.

During this very first telephone conversation he expressed his pleasure that Marshal Badoglio had known General von Rintelen

for many years and esteemed him highly. He said that on the civilian side many threads had been broken by the upheaval, and this would necessarily lead in the immediate future to even more extensive and important contacts, particularly on political matters, with General von Rintelen and his staff. He hoped that this would also lead to still further proofs of our friendship, and that as a consequence we should be able to facilitate the work of our respective chiefs in their grave responsibilities.

Many shared experiences on numerous air trips to North Africa had created a bond between me and Montezemolo, who had now been appointed to this influential position. One of the high points had been a stay of a fortnight at the headquarters in Cyrenaica in north-east Libya of Colonel-General Bastico, the Supreme Commander of all the German-Italian troops in Africa. This was in July 1942, when Rommel's army had advanced to the western bank of the Nile delta at El Alamein, and optimists believed it would be possible to continue the advance to Alexandria or Cairo. Mussolini had already flown to Africa, and was holding himself in readiness a few miles west of Bastico's headquarters for the triumphal entry into Cairo. For the same reason Marshal Cavallero, who was Chief of the Comando Supremo at the time, flew to Libya with a small staff of advisers for the purpose of influencing the operations in Libya. Rintelen, who always accompanied Cavallero on these visits to the front, had not yet recovered from a serious car accident he had had two months before, so I had to act as his deputy on this occasion. The Marshal, in strict accordance with protocol and with true Italian courtesy, insisted on my being his only companion in the cabin in the forepart of the aircraft on all his flights, particularly the day trips to the front from Bastico's headquarters. Preparations for the daily conferences at General Headquarters led to close co-operation between Montezemolo and me during those days.

An unusual and rather delicate situation arose for me during this trip to Africa. Melchiori was a member of Mussolini's suite, and he several times approached me at nightfall at Bastico's headquarters to find out what the Italian generals thought of the situation at the front, and what decisions had been reached at the conferences over which Cavallero presided. He also wanted to know my personal view of the situation. Then he would quickly hurry off to pass on what he had gleaned to Mussolini before

Cavallero reported to him later in the evening. Thus the excellent personal relations with Mussolini's political advisers and the representatives of the Italian command, thought highly desirable in principle, might easily have led in practice to difficulties as a result of this close contact at Bastico's small field headquarters at Djebel in Cyrenaica; for Mussolini was suspicious of his generals, though not nearly to the same extent as Hitler was. However, thanks to Cavallero's broad-mindedness and my excellent understanding with Montezemolo, from whom I did not conceal the conversations in which Melchiori engaged me, we were able to prevent disagreeable consequences arising from this rather remarkable by-passing of the official channels.

Montezemolo was an officer of very high quality. He had begun his military career as a reserve officer in the Engineers, before becoming a regular. His devotion to his profession and his lack of self-assertiveness were admirable. He was fair, tall, and strikingly slender. He had no interests outside his profession, and everything was subordinated to his sense of duty. The roots of his strength lay in a very happy family life. He and his wife sometimes asked whether their children's appearance and manner did not suggest they might be of German descent, and they were delighted when the answer was yes.

As a key figure in the Comando Supremo he had been totally occupied with military matters, and until his appointment to his new position he had betrayed no hint of his political views. He treated us Germans completely without prejudice and with complete frankness. He admired the German army, and promoting German–Italian co-operation was a matter of course to him during the war. If he had to make a complaint, or ask a question he thought might be embarrassing to us, he did so with extreme caution and an almost shaming modesty. Eventually he was caught up in the whirlpool of German–Italian dissension and met a tragic end; he was one of the 335 Italian hostages shot at the Adreatine caves outside Rome on 26 March 1944.

After my telephone conversation with him on 26 July, Colonel Nurra kept me in his office for a long time discussing events. Majors Marchesi and Morgantini joined us, and from time to time Lieutenant-Colonel De Francesco and Major Adam did so too. They were all genuinely delighted, and spoke of their country's liberation. They said that the Comando Supremo now had its

hands free to take sensible and necessary military steps, and there would be no more interference by military amateurs. The whole officers' corps could now breathe freely again, and it was solidly behind Badoglio. The Germans would soon be able to see for themselves that a fresh wind was blowing through the Italian army, and that its fighting spirit had improved. As a first vigorous step that had been taken they mentioned the incorporation into the ordinary armed forces of the militia, and they said that a new call-up for military service was imminent. In spite of the critical situation in Sicily, it was hoped that the Italian contribution to the joint conduct of the war would soon be so substantially increased that, in conjunction with the expected German reinforcements, as a first step at any rate further attempts at invasion by the enemy would be repulsed. Nurra thought that the Germans would now be more satisfied with Italy's military contribution.

These staff officers' delight at the downfall of the corrupt Fascist régime seemed to have produced a sudden state of euphoria that was in striking contrast to their previous attitude of deep concern at the military situation. During the days that followed we received many reports unanimously describing the prevalence of the same state of mind among Italian troops, in Italy as well as in the south of France and in the Balkans. It was reported, for instance, that the Supreme Commander West, Field-Marshal von Rundstedt, was very cordially greeted by the Italian army at Nice on 26 July. On trips lasting several days in the Italian army area the Italian officers and men had made an excellent impression on him, and he consequently believed that this army would definitely support German measures.[21]

It was out of the question that this uniformity of behaviour among Italian staffs and troops was merely a mask assumed to conceal the prospect of an early surrender. For that special instructions would have been needed. But the Italian armed forces, from the commanders inside and outside the country downwards, had no directive other than the principle announced in the proclamation by the head of government, *la guerra continua*.

At the end of the conversation Major Marchesi accompanied me to the door of the Comando Supremo building and whispered in my ear: 'I can imagine there is now a great deal for which you envy us.'

[21] Ktb. OKW, pp. 845 and 872.

At the end of the Badoglio government's first day we had obtained at any rate some glimpses into how the upheaval had come about and how the new government was setting about its task. But vital questions remained unanswered, and in many respects the first grave doubts about future developments arose. The insights we had obtained primarily concerned the downfall of the Fascist régime. Even Ambassador von Mackensen recognized its irreversibility. His telegram dated 26 July, 11.30 p.m. ended with the sentence: 'How far the inner decline of the Fascist Party had in fact progressed seems to me to be shown by the fact that, as today's events have shown, it silently vanished from the scene.'[22]

It cannot have been easy for him so plainly to admit that he had so grossly over-estimated the strength of Mussolini's and the party's position only the day before.

The most important of the questions that now loomed was the attitude of the King and the new government to their German ally and the further conduct of the war. The senior civilian and military representatives of Germany in Italy had to form a reliable view of the situation as quickly as possible.

General von Rintelen devoted himself tirelessly to the problem, and made use of all available sources to fill in the picture. After I had reported my conversations at the Comando Supremo that evening, a first attempt at an analysis was made. The starting-point was Badoglio's public declaration that the war was to continue. It could be asked why he had devoted only three words in his proclamation to this uncommonly important matter. It might perhaps seem suspicious that there had been no fuller and more vigorous reference to the defence of the homeland and its war aims. On the other hand, the proclamation as a whole was very short and succinct. Also it could be assumed that at a moment of upheaval and general uncertainty the King and Badoglio had deliberately refrained from using bellicose language to a people that were hungry for peace. Such language might perhaps have jeopardized the spontaneous support the new government needed in order to launch itself.

Kesselring and Rintelen had concluded from their conversation with Badoglio on the afternoon of 26 July that for the time being he intended no change in foreign policy, and that he was concerned to increase Italy's military effort.[23] In his memoirs Kessel-

[22] A.A. Pol. Arch., Italien, Vol. 14, No. 72463.   [23] Ktb. OKW, p. 840.

ring confirms the obvious good will of all the Italian commanders with whom he was in official contact.[24]

On the afternoon of 26 July Admiral Löwisch, the German Naval Attaché in Rome, called on Admiral Riccardi, the Commander-in-Chief of the Italian navy, and he too said it was obvious that Italy would continue to abide by her obligations under the alliance. He concluded his telegram on his conversation with Admiral Riccardi as follows: 'There is no doubt in my mind that Admiral Riccardi is convinced that the change from the Duce to Badoglio will result in no obstacles to mutual confidence in joint continuation of the struggle.'[25] A similar view was formed by Vice-Admiral Ruge, who was the head of a German liaison staff at the Italian naval command. He was asked to report on the changed situation in Italy by Grand-Admiral Dönitz, and replied on 27 July: 'The new government is trying to establish itself and has taken positive steps that show that it is determined to continue the war.'[26]

In spite of all these indications and assurances, we never imagined that Italy would continue the war for long in the way desired by the German leadership. It was no longer in a position to do so. To meet the German requirements, the last Italian soldier would have had to be killed and the last Italian village turned into a battle-ground. That was something that no responsible government could accept. The only question was how and when Italy would try to extricate herself. As we could safely assume that the Italian government and military leaders had no clear ideas on the subject yet themselves, the question had to be left open for the time being.

Doubts and fears about the future of German–Italian co-operation were roused by the first reactions from German headquarters on 26 July. Telephone communication with Berlin and the German High Command had been restored since the early hours of the morning, but those to whom we spoke, both in the Foreign Ministry and at the Army General Staff, were extremely reserved. There was ice in their voices. Even those known to have a good understanding of conditions in the Mediterranean area began by adopting an entirely impersonal tone. They seemed to be trying to put a safe distance between themselves and us, as if we were living among lepers and might perhaps have been infected.

[24] Kesselring, pp. 233 and 239.   [25] A.A. Pol. Arch., Italien, Vol. 14, No. 72482.
[26] Karl Dönitz, 10 Jahre und 20 Tage, Bonn, 1958, p. 362.

It was typical that several times during the day Ribbentrop sent Ambassador von Mackensen instructions by telephone and teleprinter 'to arrest the wire-pullers'.[27]

The Foreign Minister evidently believed that there were a handful of persons in Italy who had brought about the upheaval by 'wire-pulling', for it was hardly possible for the ambassador, with the aid of Dollmann, the SS representative, Kappler, the Police Attaché, and the embassy counsellors and messengers to arrest the whole of the new government and all the Italian army commanders. The ambassador, of course, had no authority over the German troops in Italy.

Ribbentrop's order was also sent to the Police Attaché at the Embassy. Hagen describes the reactions to its arrival as follows: 'The telegram led to an outburst of sarcastic hilarity; to demonstrate the grotesqueness of the situation, Kappler ordered the whole of the embassy police force to line up in front of him. Apart from himself and his assistant, it consisted of a young detective, plus an orderly and a woman secretary. Their prospective arrestee Badoglio, however, had five divisions in and around Rome.'[28]

Thus, in Ribbentrop's view, it would be possible to reverse the situation in Italy if a few 'guilty men' were taken into German custody. There can be a few instances in the history of diplomacy in which an embassy has received instructions to commit such a glaring breach of international law as interfering forcibly in the domestic affairs of the host country.

On the evening of 26 July we already had reason to suspect that Hitler was contemplating grim counter-measures. It could be assumed, of course, that the shameful collapse of Fascism and Mussolini's sudden resignation was a severe blow to him. To him the overnight disappearance of the man whose work he had always held up as a model to his own people was a personal blow directed at him by the King and Badoglio. The collapse of the Fascist Party, which he had publicly proclaimed to be the predecessor and brother of his own party, enraged him, and he shuddered at the thought that the contagion of the Italian example might spread to Germany. It has been claimed that 25 July 1943 was an even graver blow to him than the loss of the Sixth Army

[27] A.A. Pol. Arch., Italien, Vol. 14, No. 72466, Ribbentrop's telegraphed instruction No. 458 of 26 July, No. 3524.

[28] Walter Hagen, *Unternehmen Bernhard*, Wels and Starnberg, 1955, p. 129.

at Stalingrad six months earlier. On top of that there was the suspicion that the upheaval in Italy had been brought about in order to conclude a separate peace with the British and Americans. Hitler assumed that negotiations to this end had already begun. One of his principal traits was vengefulness, and his strongest impulse was blindly to assault the new order in Italy straight away. But he had to pay regard to the fighting in Sicily and the expected allied invasion of the Italian mainland.

The curfew in Rome was strictly observed from 26 July onwards. Apart from a deplorable mistake that resulted in a sentry's firing at a car belonging to the Turkish Embassy and killing the wife of the Counsellor at the embassy, quiet prevailed in the streets. When the men of the Piave Division who examined our special passes recognized us as Germans, they greeted us with friendly remarks.

Growth of mistrust

On the morning of 27 July General Rossi, Colonel-General Ambrosio's deputy, notified the German Military Attaché that information was being received that the transfer of German troops to Sicily had ceased. Fresh units and replacements were no longer being shipped across the Straits of Messina. Similarly, at a number of places in north and central Italy the movement of German troops to the south had stopped. The Comando Supremo therefore inquired whether the Germans had made any new decision and proposed to abandon the battle for Sicily. Rintelen could only answer evasively and undertake to make inquiries. It turned out that the Supreme Commander South had in fact issued orders halting these troops movements.[29] Italian mistrust was now aroused.

At the German Embassy the second day of the Badoglio government's life was filled with lively discussions whether Fascism could be resuscitated or not. On the previous day there had been unanimous agreement that it was impossible, as had been shown by the ambassador's telegram to the effect that it had disappeared without a whimper. Two younger, Nazi-minded, embassy counsellors, and even Dollmann himself, had spontaneously admitted that the country was behind the new government. But, with the multiplication of signs of unwillingness in Germany to admit this state

[29] Ktb. OKW, p. 839.

of affairs, the ambassador and Dollmann felt themselves obliged to fall into line.

In his telegram dated 5 p.m., 27 July, Mackensen tried to cover himself in both ways. He was unquestionably correct in foreseeing in the first part of the message that Badoglio might try 'decently to extricate himself from the conditions that today still bind Italy to the side of her Axis partner', and that the Italian people would welcome all steps directed towards that end.

He added, however, that the Marshal should not be trusted, though there was no evidence of any preparations for carrying out such a plan, i.e. 'decently to extricate himself' from the obligations of the alliance. At the end of the telegram Mackensen suggested that the Italian 'boot should be so stuffed with German forces that at a given moment we could proceed to the order of the day with this *capo del governo* (head of the government) and his possible machinations'.[30]

The first part of the telegram did justice to the situation, while the stiff language at the end was influenced by information from Germany indicating that there was no intention there of accepting the changed situation in Italy.

On the afternoon of 27 July Kappler, the Police Attaché, appeared in my office. Kappler is still in an Italian prison, having been made responsible for the shooting of 335 Italian hostages at the Adreatine caves. We had met occasionally at social and official functions, and had also had a slight clash in 1942, on which occasion, however, he behaved relatively magnanimously. He rebuked me for receiving in my home the writer Joachim von Kürenberg, who was living in Italy as a refugee. He sternly pointed out that Kürenberg had been expelled from the Reich Chamber of Authors. I replied that Kürenberg was a relative of mine, and that I would not close my door to him. However, I agreed to meet him, Kappler, to the extent of undertaking not to introduce him to any Italians. Soon afterwards Kappler accused me of helping him to escape. His hotel had been surrounded, but he had 'left' shortly beforehand. Kappler said that no doubt I had warned him. I was able to assure him, perfectly truthfully, that I knew nothing whatever either about his intended arrest or his escape. Kürenberg later spent a long time in a concentration camp, and after the war added to the large number of books he had

[30] A.A. Pol. Arch., Italien, Vol. 14, Nos. 72499–501.

already written. His best-known works are his biographies of Kaiser Wilhelm II, Katharina Schratt, Johanna von Bismarck, and Carol II, but historians have not always given them their full due.

On 27 July Kappler told me that he had come to seek my views on the situation. He had received a warning order from his superior officer, the Reichsführer SS, Heinrich Himmler, instructing him to make local preparations with a view to the restoration of the Fascist régime. As he was convinced of the total collapse of the Fascist Party, he was unable to agree with this proposal. He compared the Italians to a child who had been sick after eating some nasty soup, and so could not be persuaded to swallow the same soup again. He had therefore applied for a personal interview with Himmler to explain this point of view, but in the meantime wanted my opinion, which certainly coincided with General von Rintelen's. He was in a difficult position, because in the last few hours Dollmann had made a complete volte-face, and now, after he had got over the first shock, was willing fully to support Himmler's proposed course of action. Before taking off to see Himmler he wanted the Military Attaché's backing for the stand he was going to take. He attached particular importance to this, as the Military Attaché had close contacts with the Italian personalities who were now in authority, while the ambassador, Dollmann, and he himself had had no productive sources of official information since 25 July.

I answered briefly that I unreservedly shared his negative view of the possibility of bringing Fascism back to life, and that I could only wish him complete success in his mission, both in German and Italian interests. Kappler finished by saying that he would frankly state his views to Himmler, but as an obedient official would faithfully carry out orders, whatever they might be. He promised to tell me the outcome.

Kappler and Dollmann, both of whom were immediate subordinates of Himmler, were rivals. While the former personally carried out many unpleasant duties, Dollmann fished in troubled waters in the ambassador's shadow. Kappler always had to show his colours, both to Italians and others, while Dollmann could always conceal them when it suited his purpose.

The placing of SS representatives in embassies often led to intolerable circumstances. In the Rome Embassy Dollmann was like

an evil spirit; this was inherent in his position as Himmler's official spy and the duties that devolved on him in consequence. Prince Bismarck once said in our intimate circle that we must get used to the idea that one day he would have us all arrested. When Dollmann was present at a reception, friends warned one another to keep a watch on their tongue. He had contacts with Mussolini's entourage, and especially close contacts with the Italian secret police services, as well as with radical members of the Fascist Party. He also had a certain amount of relatively limited access to circles belonging to so-called Rome society.

His chief source of information, apart from Farinacci, was Buffarini-Guidi. Buffarini was State Secretary in the Ministry of the Interior until February 1943. His reputation in the party gradually became as dubious as Farinacci's. When Hitler set up the rump republic in north Italy in the autumn of 1943, Buffarini became its Minister of the Interior, and in that unhappy, politically torn, neo-Fascist ghost state he modelled himself on Fouché; in Anfuso's opinion, he behaved like the last Renaissance Italian.[31] Dollmann, his contact man with Himmler, aided and abetted him. In 1945 he was shot.

Post-war literature has been very hard on Dollmann.[32] Walter Hagen shows conclusively how highly Himmler valued his services.[33] The editors of the revealing collection of Hitler's *Lagebesprechungen* (conferences) say on page 347 that 'the smooth intriguer' Dollmann was Himmler's personal representative in Italy in Rome from 1939 onwards and during the period of the Italian Republic of Salò was also the chief police authority in German-occupied Italy. They also describe his *Roma nazista* as a book full of dubious information, which is putting it very mildly.

In 1963 Dollmann wrote another book of the same kind, in which he succeeds in concealing from the reader for 254 pages that he was Himmler's right arm in Italy. He does not mention who his employer was, and represents his work as having been exclusively that of an interpreter put into SS uniform against his will.[34]

In the period after 25 July he was a great nuisance to us because,

[31] Anfuso, p. 92.
[32] Galeazzo Ciano, *Diario*, Milan, 1952, p. 163; Guariglia, p. 615; Wiskemann, p. 325.
[33] Walter Hagen, op. cit., p. 125.
[34] Eugen Dollmann, *Dolmetscher der Diktatoren*, Bayreuth, 1963.

in spite of his original admission that Fascism had finally collapsed, he favoured resuscitating it by force in order to fall in with Hitler's and Himmler's line.

This hampered Rintelen's efforts, which were supported by Bismarck, to secure co-operation with the Badoglio government, on the grounds that

1. Fascism could not be revived;
2. Badoglio's government accorded with the people's will;
3. There was no alternative to it if chaos in the country, in which there was a grave threat of Communism, was to be prevented;
4. It must be advantageous, when the hoped-for early end of the long-since lost war came about, if a government of honourable and distinguished personalities were in office rather than a set of opportunist neo-Fascist adventurers;[35]
5. Violent intervention in the domestic affairs of an ally would be a crime that would still further damage the German reputation.

Ambassador von Mackensen subsequently associated himself with these ideas, at least in part. In a telegram dated 3 August he conceded that, if Badoglio fell, only much weaker transitional governments could be expected, and said that the Badoglio government's energy in maintaining order in the country must be admitted. He had been assured by a man of confidence, a proven Fascist and friend of Germany, that a restoration of the Fascist Party by the force of German arms would lead to civil war, with all its consequences, and that it would primarily be the German reputation and the still unshaken respect that it enjoyed that would suffer.[36]

General von Rintelen's contacts several times a day with Badoglio or his entourage and the Comando Supremo confirmed him in his view that precipitate German intervention must be prevented at all costs.

Mutual mistrust was dangerously increased by the delay in establishing official contact between the two heads of state and the two governments. Badoglio sent his greetings to Hitler through Doertenbach on 25 July and again through Mackensen on the afternoon of the following day, but received no reply. Hitler still believed he would soon be hearing from Mussolini.

[35] Rintelen, p. 224.   [36] A.A. Pol. Arch., Italien, Vol. 15, Nos. 72771, 72774.

On 27 July Badoglio sent a telegram to Hitler, renewing his assurance that Italy would continue the war, and stating that he had written a detailed message to the Führer to be submitted to him by the Italian Military Attaché in Berlin, General Marras, and asking that the latter might therefore be received as soon as possible. Marras, however, was not received until midday on 30 July. On the afternoon of the same day a conversation took place between him and Field-Marshal Keitel, in Ribbentrop's presence.[37] The message submitted by Marras contained the proposal that an early meeting should take place between the King and Hitler. Hitler did not reply directly, but had the proposal declined through the Foreign Ministry. Ribbentrop said in his telegram that he would be prepared to meet Badoglio or Guariglia, the new Foreign Minister; a conversation at the level of heads of state could be visualized for later.[38] At the meeting with the Italians at Tarvisio on 6 August, however, the German Foreign Minister criticized the Badoglio government for not having tried quickly enough to establish contact with the German government.

A further cause for misgiving was the continual pressure the Germans put on the Italians to reveal Mussolini's whereabouts. It was intelligible that Hitler should desire to send him a message of sympathy or consolation, but both the hostile German attitude and the necessity of maintaining order in the country made it seem essential to keep his whereabouts secret for the time being. Hence neither the King nor Badoglio gave the requested information to the German Ambassador. Mussolini was to celebrate his sixtieth birthday on 29 July, and Hitler instructed first Kesselring and then Mackensen to secure the Italian government's consent to their presenting him with a luxury edition of the collected works of Nietzsche on the occasion—a graceful tribute in the circumstances. The Italian government declined the suggestion that this gift should be presented personally, but gave an assurance that it would be duly passed on. The Germans were also assured that Mussolini was well, and that the King was informed daily about the state of his health.

On 27 and 28 July there was growing excitement at the Comando Supremo at news from the northern frontier posts that unannounced German units were approaching the frontier.[39] Sharp

[37] MGFA DZ, Akte H 27/58, Tätigskeitbericht der Attaché-Abteilung, 9.8.1943.
[38] A.A. Pol. Arch., Italien, Vol. 14, No. 72688. [39] Ktb. OKW, pp. 1013–15.

protests were made by the Comando Supremo, followed by equally sharp replies from the German High Command, all of which had to be passed on by General von Rintelen. In the days that followed dissension on the subject grew more and more acute. The Italians, led by Colonel-General Ambrosio and General Roatta, expressed their great astonishment that more and more German divisions were appearing at the frontier posts, though in June and earlier in July the German leadership had solemnly reiterated that with the best will in the world it had no more divisions to spare to reinforce the front in the Mediterranean area. The Italian surprise was increased at the appearance among these German forces of the 44th Austrian Division (the Hoch- und Deutschmeister Division) and actually the Leibstandarte Adolf Hitler, which had been withdrawn from the Russian front, where heavy fighting was taking place. It was immediately obvious to the Italians that these units could have been transferred to Italy only with political purposes in mind. The final shock to the Comando Supremo was that all these troops remained in north Italy instead of being sent south to take part in the operations against the allies. The German excuse was that these troops were needed to prevent enemy landings in north Italy and to protect the Alpine passes against landings from the air.[40] The Comando Supremo could see nothing to suggest that the allies were making preparations for any such strategically misguided operations.

As the newly arrived German troops to an extent behaved as if they were in occupied territory, the Italians reacted accordingly. Orders from Rome that troop movements should be slowed down to prevent blockages in the transport system and to give time for the preparation of reception areas caused Italian frontier posts and troops to adopt a protesting attitude, which the Germans in turn construed as hostility and took offence at.

It has often been alleged that immediately after Badoglio's assumption of office the Italians occupied the fortifications on the Brenner and elsewhere; the developments we have just described partially explain these allegations. There is a cautious reference to the matter in the war diary of the German High Command. Army Group B (commanded by Field-Marshal Rommel, with headquarters then in Munich) is stated to have reported on 30 July

[40] Kurt von Tippelskirch, *Geschichte des Zweiten Weltkriegs.* Frankfurt and Bad Godesberg, 1951, p. 366.

F

that piecemeal reinforcements were being inconspicuously sent to Italian posts on the Brenner line. Also there were signs (!) that explosive charges were being delivered to fortified positions.[41]

A report dated 3 August 1943 by Strohm, the German consul-general at Bolzano, is worth mentioning in this connection. He doubted the correctness of the information that the Italians were taking steps to occupy the frontier defences with a view to blocking the passes. These were theories of the intelligence service based on the nervousness of Germans in the South Tyrol. In the instances that it had been possible to check, false conclusions had been drawn by peasants from the movements of a few Italian lorries.[42] I received corroboration then and later from staff officers of German formations in the area that the belief that the Italians were taking such measures was obviously based on the prevalent anxiety; such information did not stand up to thorough checking.

The highly significant fact remains that further developments were decisively influenced by the surprisingly rapid transfer to Italy of at least eight German divisions from France and Russia. A month earlier, when General Roatta had made an urgent plea for roughly that number of German divisions to strengthen the Axis defences in Italy, he had been told that it was out of the question. But now, following the change of government, they came pouring into Italy like an avalanche, though since 5 July there had again been heavy fighting on the German eastern front and the German commanders there were urgently appealing for reinforcements.

To their further alarm, the Italians discovered that it had been secretly agreed that the command of all these troops and those that were to follow was to be given to Field-Marshal Rommel. They took this as an unfriendly sign. They expected a tough attitude to Italy on Rommel's part, as in the retreat in North Africa during the previous winter a grave deterioration had taken place in the relations between him and the Italian leadership.

All these German measures vitally affected, and above all accelerated, the later decision of the Badoglio government to establish contact with the allies. Its hopes of arriving at a satisfactory agreement with the Germans over bringing the war to an end dwindled away, and it felt directly threatened by them.

At about midday on 28 July Lieutenant-Colonel Jandl, who had

[41] Ktb. OKW, p. 860.   [42] A.A. Pol. Arch., Italien, Vol. 15, No. 72815.

been in Rome for some time to familiarize himself with military attaché work, appeared in my room. After carrying out a special mission, he was to become my successor in the autumn of that year, and later he became liaison officer with Mussolini at the latter's so-called seat of government on Lake Garda. Jandl had just been driving through the city, and the question he fired at me was whether it was true that Hitler was dead. When I replied that I knew nothing about it, he looked disappointed and told me what had happened. He had been on his way to present himself to the attachés' department at the War Ministry, and therefore, contrary to the usual custom of the Military Attaché's staff, was wearing uniform. He said that in the Piazza Esedra his car had been held up by an excited crowd yelling: *Hitler è morto! Viva la Germania! Viva l'Italia! Viva la pace!* He had been cheered and mobbed like a victorious commander returning from the war. He had had no alternative but to smile graciously in every direction, and he had not been able to drive on for several minutes. The same performance had been repeated with the same enthusiasm near the church of Santa Maria Maggiore. Outside the Embassy many passers by had waved to him and called out: *Hitler è morto!*

An uninterrupted flow of telephone inquiries set in from German offices and private individuals in Rome. My wife telephoned from a shop, and said she had just met the Spanish Deputy Military Attaché, who had told her about Hitler's alleged death, and had significantly invited her to join him in drinking an *apéritif* in the Via Vittorio Veneto.

The German railway transport officer at the Termini station, where a trainload of German troops had just arrived, rang up and asked for instructions; he was almost in a state of frenzy because of the unrestrainable demonstrations of joy being indulged in on the platform by Italian and German troops. The Italians cheered and embraced the Germans as they got out of the train. The Germans did not know what it was all about. Some thought that such a reception was normal in Italy, most did not understand what the Italians were shouting at them, and others joined in the jubilation. When confirmation arrived from Berlin that it was nothing but a wild rumour, the excitement quickly died away. The incident might well have had unpleasant consequences for those Germans who accepted the news prematurely and with visible satisfaction. The Italian town commandant of Rome had to send armoured

reconnaissance vehicles to patrol the main streets to break up other demonstrations. Also the population had again to be reminded of the seriousness of the situation.[43]

Signs multiplied that Hitler was seriously planning to liberate Mussolini and restore the Fascist Party to power. The cold shoulder shown to the Badoglio government, German troop movements to and in Italy, the suddenly diminution of German interest in the fighting in Sicily, and the insistent inquiries about Mussolini's whereabouts, all pointed in the same direction.

In view of our anxiety to prevent reckless and dangerous actions, I suggested to General von Rintelen on the afternoon of 28 July that an attempt should be made to persuade Mussolini to write personally to Hitler. The idea arose from my knowledge of the contents of the letter that Mussolini had written to Badoglio on the evening of 25 July. As Mussolini in that letter had acknowledged the change that had taken place in Italy, wished Badoglio success, and declared his loyalty to the King, he might be expected to express himself in more or less the same terms in a letter to Hitler. The contents of his letter to Badoglio were known to the German leadership, so it could be assumed that if he wrote to Hitler he would take the same line.

What Badoglio's attitude in the matter would be was not easy to foresee, but it could be assumed that he might hope for a moderation of Hitler's attitude as a result and, in view of all that was known about Hitler's reactions to events in Italy so far, the attempt could be expected to be welcome to him for that reason. At least it might gain him valuable time in which to consolidate his government.

It seemed reasonable to expect that a change of attitude on Hitler's part would be more likely if he received a letter from Mussolini, manifestly not dictated under pressure, asking or actually appealing to him to continue to co-operate with Italy in spite of his resignation as head of the Italian government.

I mentioned the possibility of my putting this idea to Montezemolo.

Rintelen had two reservations. He thought it would be a very high-handed action on the part of a Military Attaché, without the knowledge of his superiors, to put such a proposal, directly or by way of the Comando Supremo, to the head of the Italian govern-

[43] Ibid., Vol. 14, Nos. 72584–6.

ment, for it would constitute a very definite intervention in the foreign policy of both countries. Nevertheless it deserved serious consideration for, in view of the disastrous implications of the steps now being discussed in Germany, there must be no jibbing at taking an unconventional step if it held out good hope of success.

He also had doubts about Badoglio's willingness to ask Mussolini for what amounted to a letter of recommendation, so to speak, to Hitler. The Marshal was by no means free of vanity, and he might reject such a suggestion out of sensitivity, or perhaps actually regard it as presumptuous.

I clung to the hope, however, that Badoglio would subject his personal pride to the possible great potential utility of the step. It was regrettable from this point of view that no German personality had access to Mussolini, and hence that there was no way of by-passing Badoglio. Had Field-Marshal Kesselring, for instance, been permitted to hand over the German birthday present to Mussolini, he might well have made the suggestion.

After briefly considering the matter, General von Rintelen sent for me again. I always admired the balance he kept between duly weighing up situations and making decisions. Without either hurrying or wasting time, he reached his decision and considered the ways and means of implementing it.

On this occasion he decided that the attempt should be made. In his view, however, the Comando Supremo should be left out of it. Also, for the sake of prudence, any direct approach to Badoglio or Montezemolo should be avoided. Major Gericke, who was on friendly terms with the Badoglio family, should therefore be asked to communicate the suggestion in the way that seemed best to him. In no circumstances must the matter be mentioned to anyone else.

At Gericke's suggestion I discussed the matter with him at his flat at 7 p.m. that evening. His final observation was that he felt himself free to make use of his wife's help if this should turn out to be advisable or necessary.

Two days later he told me that Badoglio apparently felt unable to accept the proposal. He took the view that Hitler already knew the text of the letter that Mussolini had written to him, Badoglio, and that was enough. If Mussolini wrote to Hitler, he could not declare his loyalty to the King and the new government more plainly than he had done already.

Unfortunately Badoglio seemed to underestimate the psychological effect on Hitler of a personal letter from Mussolini. Mussolini meant a great deal to him, and he was ready to pay regard to him. At conferences after the Italian upheaval he frequently asked why he had been given no news of him. He would gladly have postponed decisions until hearing from him. 'I am only waiting for news of what the Duce says.'[44]

It is not only Hitler's own words that entitle one to suppose that a personal letter from Mussolini might have been useful; Ribbentrop's complaints at the German–Italian meeting at Tarvisio on 6 August 1943, to which we shall return in due course, point in the same direction. The German Foreign Minister complained to Guariglia, his Italian colleague, about the way in which the change in Italy 'had taken place in relation to their German ally'. When Guariglia asked what was meant by this, Ribbentrop said that no communication had been received from Mussolini himself.[45]

The evening of 28 July was especially interesting. Montezemolo, who had been available only for short telephone conversations during the day, came to my flat, and a long discussion took place. I also invited Major Morgantini, of the Comando Supremo, with whom I had established terms of friendship three years earlier, when I was a guest at the Italian Military Academy at Turin. He had a German wife.

Montezemolo began by describing how he had been unexpectedly called from his bed early on the morning of 26 July to take up the position of *chef de cabinet* to Badoglio. He gave another humorous description of all the difficulties involved in scraping together in a few hours the staff necessary to man the office of a head of government, besides all the other arrangements that had to be made. He said it was intelligible that the sudden and swift collapse of the Fascist régime should have caused surprise, and certainly also consternation at first, in Germany. But, after the first three days of the new government's life, anxiety that signs of disintegration might be going to appear in Italy must have been dissipated. Italy now at last had a war cabinet that would hold the nation together during the undoubtedly difficult time that lay

[44] Lage, p. 313.
[45] A.A. Pol. Arch., Büro Reichsminister, Handakten Dolmetscher Schmidt, 1943, Part II, No. 48798.

ahead. There would be no more treating war profiteers and the like with kid gloves.

Montezemolo went on to enumerate measures that showed the government's determination to measure up to the requirements of the war situation. As a more outward sign of this, he mentioned the severity of the steps taken by the government under the state of emergency, which the Fascist government had never summoned up courage to impose. To the army's dismay, it had always shilly-shallied and taken half-measures. But Badoglio had already put the Post Office and the railways under military administration, imposed severe restrictions on civilian travel, declared three-quarters of the country to be a war area, and incorporated the militia into the army.

The army, the navy, and the air force were solidly behind Badoglio. Before 25 July they had been approaching the point of disintegration. It must be frankly admitted that the fighting spirit of the Italian troops in Sicily had been a disgrace to the country and a grave humiliation in the face of their ally, but this total failure had been primarily attributable to the estrangement of the officers' corps from the Fascist leadership, for which it no longer wanted to fight. All the signs indicated that the fighting spirit of the armed forces was now greatly improving.

Badoglio appreciated that the German leaders had not been able to rid themselves of the idea that Fascism had succumbed to a surprise attack but was by no means totally broken. It could only be hoped that eye-witness reports by the German representatives in Rome would lead to an early correction of this mistake. From the party ideological point of view, there was no need for anyone in Germany to have the slightest anxiety about the fate of veteran Fascists. The Badoglio government had no thought of reprisals, though many voices were raised for this among the people. The times were far too serious for the government to burden itself unnecessarily with the settling of scores in the domestic field. All Fascists who were not guilty of any punishable offence had been left at their posts.

The irrevocability of the self-liquidation of the Fascist Party was strikingly illustrated by the fact that the former party leaders all supported the Badoglio government. Mussolini himself had offered it his services in his letter of 25 July, and the former almost omnipotent party secretary Carlo Scorza had written to Badoglio on 26 July asking for employment.

I knew from Prince Bismarck that Ribbentrop still attached great importance to Scorza's taking refuge in Germany, because he wanted to make him a leading figure in counter-action against the Badoglio régime. It would inevitably be a bitter disappointment to the German Foreign Minister and to Mackensen, who had taken so much trouble to try to lure him to Germany, to discover that he supported the new government. So I asked Montezemolo whether he was sure that there was no misunderstanding in this instance.

Another example that he gave me was Testa, the former Prefect of Fiume and the last special plenipotentiary for Sicily. This high official was also urgently appealing for employment; in fact he refused to budge from Badoglio's antechamber. Testa, as we knew very well, had had the reputation of being a fanatical Fascist and one of the pillars of the party.

As an exception Montezemolo briefly and contemptuously mentioned Farinacci, and he cautiously and tactfully indicated Badoglio's regret that the German Ambassador had committed an 'unfriendly act' against Italy for the sake of such a worthless individual. It could only be hoped that he would quickly be seen through by all those who were now having dealings with him in Germany. It would be deplorable if this vengeful slanderer succeeded in gaining the ear of leading German personalities.

At this time we did not yet know that Farinacci's unreliability had been recognized after his very first conversations at German headquarters. So for the time being I was unable to dispel Montezemolo's anxieties in the matter.

He also briefly referred to the incident on the evening of 25 July, when Badoglio had not succeeded in informing the German Ambassador of the change of government at the earliest possible moment because the latter had several times declared himself to be unavailable.

He went on to say that the government greatly deplored the fact that in the days after the upheaval the Italian press had not been sufficiently informed, and hence had reported matters so inadequately. This, like other aesthetic blemishes, was attributable solely to the fact that the government had entered office so unprepared. When this was borne in mind, it was a cause for satisfaction that there had not been a larger number of undesirable occurrences. The Minister Rocco, who had taken the oath of office that afternoon, had now received instructions regarding the

censorship of the press in accordance with wartime needs and the provision of appropriate 'guidance' for it.

Montezemolo spoke with concern of the fact that Italian pleasure at the political change had heen clouded by the cool and to an extent also actually surly attitude of the German ally. This made Marshal Badoglio's task immensely more difficult, and their common aims were not served thereby. Party political considerations should not lead to any neglect of the alliance in this grave crisis of the war. At this point I intervened to say that the German leadership regarded the question whether the Badoglio government wished to depart from its previous foreign policy as more important than political or ideological differences. This remark was not based on my view of Hitler's attitude, but it seemed to me to be desirable to make it, in order to lead the conversation with Badoglio's *chef de cabinet*, who was exceptionally well informed at this time, to more fundamental questions. Montezemolo's spontaneous reply was that the new government had not yet even discussed problems of foreign policy, let alone made decisions on them. Sufficient evidence for this was the fact that Guariglia, the newly appointed Foreign Minister, had not yet arrived in Rome. It was obvious that for the time being everything was going on as before. So that there should be full clarity in the matter, it was urgently necessary that a German–Italian meeting at the highest level should be arranged as quickly as possible, and Badoglio had officially proposed this to the Reich government. At this meeting, after examination of the military situation, the consequences for the future conduct of the war must be jointly drawn. Hence it was to be hoped that normal contact between the two governments would be quickly restored.

Montezemolo, as was to be expected of an Italian senior staff officer, spoke of Badoglio with great respect. He confessed with a smile, however, that the Marshal was well known for always sticking very stubbornly to his views. He must therefore certainly be regarded as rather difficult to negotiate with. He was nearly seventy-two, and had accepted office at the King's bidding without ambition and only out of a sense of duty, and a certain rigidity due to age must certainly be taken into account.

Next morning, 29 July, I communicated the contents of this conversation to General von Rintelen and Ambassador von Mackensen. They were specially interested in Scorza's having gone over to

Badoglio, a fact of which Mackensen was previously unaware. At midday on 28 July Mackensen had telegraphed that he was going to have Scorza rescued 'in the way you know of'[46] but on the same evening he was told by an intermediary that Scorza created an impression of total apathy. The ambassador telegraphed to this effect to Berlin at 1.40 a.m., adding that he must 'unfortunately' revise his opinion of Scorza. He ended his telegram on a note of superfluously grandiloquent resignation: 'The only men whom we can use at this moment are those willing to sacrifice themselves to the Duce, as the men of the March on Rome could and did. They seem to have vanished from the scene.'[47]

On 29 July Mackensen sent a further telegram, based on the information given me by Montezemolo, that Scorza had written to Badoglio offering him his services.[48] This piece of information was repeated in a long telegram signed by Mackensen and dispatched at 9 p.m. on 29 July, reporting the important points arising out of my conversation with Montezemolo.[49]

Ribbentrop regarded the news about Scorza as incredible and false, and had a telephone message sent informing us that we must not 'allow ourselves to be taken in by such rubbish'.

In the spring of 1944 Scorza was tried by a neo-Fascist court at Parma. He was charged with having behaved in an anti-Fascist manner when the change of government took place in July 1943. As he had not voted for Grandi's anti-Mussolini resolution at the meeting of the Grand Council, the charge was based primarily on the letter he wrote to Badoglio on 26 July, that is, the letter mentioned by Montezemolo in which Ribbentrop refused to believe. At the trial it was referred to as the 'capitulation letter', and it was reproduced in all the newspapers in north Italy.[50] Montezemolo was not in the habit of spreading false information.

As more German troops entered north Italy unannounced on 29 July, General von Rintelen had another day of wearing inquiries and reassurances exchanged between the German High Command and the Comando Supremo. It was clear from the attitude of several generals and staff officers that it was only in the face of superior German force that they ended by modifying, without withdrawing, their protests at these hurried transfers to Italy of German troops. Though the opinion was rightly expressed that a

---

[46] A.A. Pol. Arch., Italien, Vol. 14, No. 72574.   [47] Ibid., No. 72589.
[48] Ibid., No. 72612.   [49] Ibid., Nos. 72615–17.   [50] Deakin, pp. 734 f. and 769.

task 'as difficult as it was painful' devolved on General von Rintelen in this respect.[51]

I again met General Castellano that morning, and he asked me into his room. Walking backwards and forwards in his temperamental Sicilian way, he began the conversation with the words: *E voi? Non abbiamo dato un esempio? Aspettiamo!* ('And what about you? Have we not set an example? We are waiting!') What he was hinting at was plain enough. I had had a number of hints of the same type during the past few days from Marchesi and other Italian friends. Even our cook Maria repeated daily: *Quando fate lo stesso?* ('When are you going to do the same?') I tried to read Castellano a lecture on the difference between the Fascist and the Nazi régimes, and warned him against a false appreciation of the situation, but he shook his head incredulously. He made the typical Italian gesture of pressing his thumb against his fingertips and muttered that he could not understand why the great German people was rushing headlong to ruin. Then he quickly changed the subject.

Even without these Italian hints we had been continually preoccupied since 25 July with the thought of the possible repercussions in Germany and in other countries allied to or occupied by her. But the days and evenings were so taken up with dealing with messages and incidents and negotiations with the Italians that for the time being there was no chance of discussing the subject with General von Rintelen, Bismarck, and Doertenbach. But we all nourished the hope, that had been mentioned by Gisevius at the beginning of July, that something similar would happen in Germany that would hasten the end of the war. That was another reason why the new government in Italy enjoyed our sympathy. We wanted the way to a new order based on liberty and democracy to be opened for our country too. Italy had set out on that path under the auspices of its hereditary constitutional monarchy, even though it was hampered by the many demands of the wartime situation.[52]

[51] Warlimont, p. 384.

[52] It has been claimed that a growth of aversion from the House of Savoy had taken place in broad sections of the population, in anti-Fascist groups, and among traditional republicans. The King was said to have put Fascism in the saddle and then 'betrayed' it to save himself. The compromised system was said to be anti-Fascist only in name and to be determined to continue to oppose genuine democratic republicanism. In my opinion these developments took place at a later stage.

Seen from Rome, the question whether the change in Italy would serve as an example and a beacon to others was influenced by the picture painted by visitors from Germany.

In 1942 and 1943 almost every conversation with these visitors created the impression that the belief that Germany's war prospects were hopeless was becoming more and more widespread. Those who expressed themselves on this matter in private conversation revealed pessimism and even despair about the disastrous German leadership. To quote only a few examples, that was the impression left behind by Admiral Canaris, General Fellgiebel, and Lieutenant-Colonel Count Stauffenberg. Even General Warlimont, the Deputy Chief of the Army General Staff, and Lieutenant-Colonel Fett, who accompanied him, spoke without illusions about this war that exceeded Germany's strength.

One of these frequent visitors to Rome was General von Senger und Etterlin, whose adjutant I had been in the last years before the war, when he was in command of Cavalry Regiment No. 3 at Göttingen; he made a reputation as a writer on military matters both at home and abroad after the war. On 25 July 1943 he was chief of the German liaison staff with the Italian commander in Sicily. In his book *Krieg in Europa* he mentions that at the time it was possible to hope that events in Italy would have repercussions that might spare the German people their final agony. He says that from the purely military point of view it was foolish and mistaken to write off Italy as an ally after 25 July. He compared the two allies to climbers on a vertical wall. If one fell, it put such a strain on the rope that the other could climb no farther.[53]

The concern and anxiety felt by German senior officers, in so far as they were not close collaborators of Hitler's, with the result that they unintelligibly continually succumbed to his spell, or commanders engaged in heavy battle, with the result that their attention was completely absorbed by their own sector, was typically represented by Colonel, later General, Ernst-Günther Baade. Before the war he had been the senior squadron commander of Cavalry Regiment No. 3 under Senger. When Hitler in the middle of the war broke with the traditional rule by which two chaplains, a Catholic and a Protestant, were allotted to each division, Baade said in his next periodic report that the fighting spirit of the troops under his command had been very adversely affected by this

[53] Frido von Senger und Etterlin, *Krieg in Europa*, Cologne, 1960, p. 189.

measure. More than 80 per cent of his men were practising Christians. An intermediate command inquired whether he would not prefer to withdraw this expression of opinion, which would cause offence in the highest quarters. Baade insisted on its remaining, whereupon he was relieved of his command.

In July 1943 an energetic and resourceful commander was needed for the Straits of Messina, because the security of transport across the straits was vital to the defence of the island, and the appointment was given to Baade. Thus he was in Italy on 25 July, and hoped it would serve as an example in Germany, and in particular that it would have a rousing effect on senior officers. He had previously discussed with like-minded officers a project for overthrowing the Nazi régime based on the idea that the anti-aircraft units stationed round the cities of Germany were strong enough to seize power.

I myself came into contact with this project again when I was invited to a confidential conversation on 5 November 1943 at the battle headquarters of the Reich Air Fleet at the Reich Sports Field in Berlin. The successful fighter pilot Colonel Freiherr von Maltzahn, with whom I had been on terms of close friendship since we went through pilot training together in 1930, took me to his commander, Colonel-General Weise. Maltzahn had previously told me of the intention of this officer and his closest colleagues to make preparations for a revolt by the Luftwaffe and anti-aircraft units under their command against the Nazi leadership with a view to bringing about an end of the war. Weise asked whether I would be willing to initiate one or two reliable officials at the Foreign Ministry into the project; with their aid contact with the Foreign Ministry could be quickly established when the time came. I agreed, and in the evening I got into touch with Doertenbach, who had now been transferred from Rome to the Foreign Ministry in Berlin.

After my introduction to Colonel-General Weise, Maltzahn, and Colonel Falck, the No. 1a staff officer of the Air Fleet, asked whether in my opinion it might be possible to win over Field-Marshal Rommel to the project; they would very much have liked to have had this vigorous commander with his great reputation on their side. My answer at the time was no. During the operations in Italy he had shown himself to be still a henchman of Hitler's.

A noticeable change in his attitude came about only after he took command of an army group in northern France in 1944. Lieutenant-General Speidel, who was his Chief of Staff there, noticeably influenced and accelerated the change of heart that was taking place in him.

The revolutionary plans concocted at the air fleet command at the Reich Sports Field were soon dropped, however, as Colonel-General Weise was suddenly relieved of his command. I have no idea whether it was suspicion that led to this important change of personnel.

This atmosphere that prevailed in 1943 makes it intelligible that what we were told by visitors to Rome should have made it seem not unreasonable for us to expect that events in Italy might influence developments in Germany. But we found it very hard to decide whether a consolidation or a rapid collapse of the Badoglio government would tend to bring about a quicker end of the war. The former might spread political infection to other countries allied to or occupied by Germany and also to Germany itself. This was likely to be the case particularly if Italy, as was to be expected, soon urged its ally to bring the fighting to an end and make peace. In the second event an immediate total withdrawal of Italy, in the opinion of General von Senger, for instance, must obviously lead to a deterioration of the German military position and an acceleration of allied operations. The steps that Hitler had taken, particularly the rapid transfer to Italy of many German divisions, had for the time being led to a position in between these two extremes. Hitler wanted to prolong the war at all costs, and from that point of view it could not be denied that the best way had been chosen. Those who were opposed to a prolongation of the war and hoped that it might be brought to an end in co-operation with Italy must therefore want the Badoglio government to remain in the saddle as long as possible. The beginnings of a no longer totalitarian state in Hitler-dominated Europe should be saved from premature collapse; they should at least, if at all possible, act as a flash of lightning and a stimulus to the forces of opposition.

When I returned to Germany after the end of my work in Rome in the autumn of 1943, I had to admit that my ideas about the mood in Germany were wrong. From a distance it was not always possible accurately to assess the impact of propaganda and terror. Having grown used to free and open conversation with Italians for

several years, one's vision of the incomparably more difficult situation of the German population was disturbed. Also the open speech of German visitors to Rome unconsciously created an exaggerated impression of the growth of criticism and opposition in Germany.

After returning from Italy, I saw how firmly the population, after years of exposure to diabolically skilful propaganda, continued to believe in every new argument produced to show the certainty of victory. Local group leaders and block wardens, both in town and in country, kept vigilant watch. Also the régime could unfortunately rely on the younger officers, who had passed through the Hitler Youth and had no memories of 1916–18. Many generals pointed out that, if they revolted, these officers would not follow them. This was certainly a great obstacle, and a contrast to the conditions that preceded the change of régime in Italy.

Operation Student

Before I describe the events that made 31 July 1943 a black day for me, let me describe a brief episode that occurred on the previous day. On the afternoon of 30 July SS Sturmbannführer Wenner, Dollmann's colleague, came to see me, accompanied by two powerfully built young men wearing civilian jackets over boots and dark uniform trousers. Without beating about the bush, he asked for a list of the private addresses of all the Italian senior officers in Rome employed at the Comando Supremo or on the General Staffs of the three services. He also asked me for a sketch-map of all the barracks in Rome, with details of the units quartered in them. I said I would submit his request to General von Rintelen but, so far as private addresses were concerned, I could already inform him that we had no information about them other than that contained in the Rome telephone book, to which he already had access. We had no information about what units were in which barracks; collecting such information was no part of a Military Attaché's duties. We filed all information that became known to us through appropriate channels or by chance, and it was no part of our duties to do more than that, e.g. slink about with a camera concealed under our coats prying into the affairs of the host country. Wenner took his departure, remarking that he would inform Dollmann of my reply. His companions cast notably inquisitive glances into all the corners of my office. They were

members of the Skorzeny task force that later—in September 1943—rescued Mussolini from captivity on the Gran Sasso d'Italia.

When I told General von Rintelen of Wenner's visit, he wanted to know exactly what I had answered. When I told him he nodded, indicating his agreement with what I had said, and behaved as if that was the end of the matter so far as he was concerned.

On the morning of 31 July he told me that he had something very serious indeed to tell me. Since the day after the change of régime in Italy, that is, since 26 July, Hitler had been seriously planning to overthrow the Badoglio government by force. The strictest orders had been given that the number of those in the know must be kept to a minimum. 'There is no need for me to say how I feel towards this project', he said. 'A conference on the matter, limited to a small number of persons, has just been arranged for this afternoon at Field-Marshal Kesselring's headquarters. I cannot go, because I have to deal immediately with the dispute between the German High Command and the Comando Supremo about the entry into Upper Italy of the 305th Division. So you will have to go to Frascati to attend the conference, and that is why I must let you into the secret. Everything else you will hear on the spot.'[54] In accordance with specific instructions, Rintelen made me sign a document acknowledging the obligation of secrecy in the matter.

I arrived at Field-Marshal Kesselring's headquarters at Frascati at 3 p.m. Others present in the big conference room of the Supreme Commander South were the Luftwaffe General Student and Major General Westphal, Kesselring's Chief of Staff. The naval Captain Neubauer, of Kesselring's staff, attended the conference at intervals; he evidently had other things to attend to as well.

Kesselring began by saying that Hitler had ordered an attack on the Italian army and the Italian government in Rome in order to put Fascism back into the saddle. All preparations were subject to the highest degree of secrecy. As a precautionary measure Hitler's orders had been communicated verbally by an officer of his headquarters (this was Captain Junge of the German navy).[55] Nothing about the project was subsequently to be put in writing. Today's conference was concerned exclusively with the attack on the government, of which the Luftwaffe General Student was to be in charge. Preparations were to be accelerated, to enable the

[54] Ktb. OKW, p. 864 f.   [55] Ibid., p. 837.

operation to be carried out when the prearranged code-word was given on or after 2 August, thus in three days' time. Kesselring then asked General Student to outline his plan and state his requirements for carrying it through.

Student, wearing a white uniform jacket, was obviously very conscious of the great importance of the task for which he had been selected by the Führer. His orders were to take into custody the leading Italian personalities suspected of 'treachery against Germany' and to prepare for the liberation of the Duce. He had at his disposal for this purpose a strong contingent of the 2nd Parachute Division, which had been airlifted from France. He could also draw on the 3rd Panzer Grenadier Division, which had been stationed for some time north of Rome. Of the troops under the command of the Supreme Commander he also needed infantry units from the Naples area and above all a large number of lorries for the motorization of the parachute troops. He had to report on the state of the preparations next morning at the Führer's headquarters in East Prussia. At the present conference the details of the operation in Rome had once more to be checked and settled.

Student, who made this speech standing, put on his glasses and drew a piece of paper from his pocket. He was going to arrest the King and Queen, obviously in a night-time *coup de main*, as well as the Prince and Princess of Piedmont, and have them taken to Germany. He had also been specifically ordered to take from their beds at least two of the children of the heir and heiress to the throne. The list he had been given included about forty more persons, beginning with Badoglio, Guariglia, and Ambrosio. He read out the Italian names slowly, and generally his pronunciation was quite unintelligible.

These were painful moments. Nearly all the individuals he mentioned were very well known to me, and they were all authoritative personalities of a sovereign state. The fate that they could expect in Germany was not difficult to imagine.

I was sitting next to General Westphal and, while Student painfully reeled off name after name, I could see through the wide-open window the panorama of the Roman Campagna stretching out below all the way to the domes of all the Roman churches. Frascati is on a height, and in the glittering sunshine this small world that had played such a huge part in history lay apparently

G

peacefully at our feet. The scene conflicted horribly with the mean
human hostilities that were being plotted here.

There could be no doubt in my mind about where this list of
intended victims came from. It could have come only from Dollmann, because the names of Colonna and Vitetti appeared on it.
These families had talked disparagingly of Dollmann for years.
Vitetti, whom we have already mentioned in connection with the
meeting at Klessheim earlier in the year, was head of a department in the Foreign Ministry. According to Student's list, he was
to be arrested because his wife was an American and a Jewess; she
was therefore to be taken into custody and sent to Germany. The
list included the names of about twelve generals belonging to the
Comando Supremo and the army, navy, and air staffs. Their
names were given in strict accordance with rank.

When Student had finished, Westphal said that steps would
have to be taken immediately to ensure that the infantry units
from Naples and the motor transport that had already been ordered
for the parachute troops should arrive in good time. But delays
must be expected, as transport was short; it would have to be
taken from that required by the troops in south Italy. Student
bridled at this, and insisted that this operation specially ordered
by the Führer must be given overriding priority. When Kesselring also pointed out that the time-factor played a part, Student
flared up again and said: 'We cannot put difficulties in the way
of an order by the Führer.' These exchanges were of great value
to me, because they enabled me to detect that Kesselring and
Westphal secretly opposed the enterprise.

Student said it was important that the homes of the persons to be
taken into custody should be checked. In regard to the royal
family, everything was straightforward. A way into the Villa
Savoia would be forced with the aid of assault ladders. Could the
correctness of the addresses of the other persons stated in the
Embassy list be relied on?

Student looked at me inquiringly. I said there was no doubt that
the Italians were displaying a certain anxiety about the possibility
of such action by the Germans. It was possible that houses might
be guarded, and that use was being made of alternative accom-
modation.

I felt justified in making this remark in order to help Kesselring
and Westphal, who were obviously playing for time. Also it had

happened to come to my knowledge on the previous day that General Rossi, the Deputy Chief of the Comando Supremo, had had a room made ready at his headquarters so that he could stay there overnight.

Student grew indignant. So Italian suspicions had been roused, and a secret had been betrayed in the most outrageous manner.

General Westphal said there was a rumour that something might have leaked out by way of the Vatican.

Student said that he now regarded in a different light the information brought him by his reconnaissance troops about the strengthening of the military guard at the Villa Savoia. The assault party would have to be strengthened and the list of addresses carefully rechecked.

The strength of the Italian troops in and around Rome was then discussed. General Westphal gave a warning against underestimating their strength. I had the impression that he rounded the figures out in an upward direction in order to make the operation look difficult, if not impossible, and at the same time wanted to save German troops from possible losses as a result of careless planning.

Field-Marshal Kesselring intervened from time to time supporting the observations of his Chief of Staff.

I was able to make some contributions to the discussion to the same effect in regard to the various barracks in Rome. I pointed out, for instance, that I drove daily past the biggest complex of barracks in the city, known as 'Macao', the former quarters of the Genova Cavalry Regiment, and during the past few days had noticed an increased number of vehicles going in and coming out, as well as light tanks.

Student left with an angry expression on his face. His parting shot was that he would clear up everything at headquarters in East Prussia next day.

After his departure, Field-Marshal Kesselring, looking very dejected and aged, said to Westphal and me: 'This is how one becomes a bandit chief.'

He kept me for a few minutes to discuss another matter. Then he walked out with me, because he had to go and see Badoglio. Outside he shook hands with me, sighed deeply, and said something that remains firmly in my memory: 'I never thought that I should end my fine military career like this.'

By previous arrangement I then went to see General Westphal in his office. In the presence of Lieutenant-Colonel Berlin he expressed his indignation at the project known by the code-name of Operation Student. In the confusion arising from the many plans that were made against the Italians it was also sometimes known as Operation Black.[56]

General Westphal told me something of the previous history of the affair. He showed me carbon copies of messages that had been exchanged. On 27 July Kesselring had commented to the German High Command on the instructions for Operation Student imparted to him on the previous day by Captain Junge. He had asked for it to be postponed. He said that, in view of the existing transport and supply crisis, immediate carrying out of the operation might lead to a loss of the German divisions in Sicily and south Italy. The disruption of communications and blockages at the ports that must be expected would also contribute to this, and he said that the arrival of further German divisions in Italy should be awaited. He also said that the project would turn against us all those Italians who were still well-disposed towards us.[57]

Westphal told me that Field-Marshal Kesselring had also expressed his opposition to the operation in a personal interview with Göring, but had met with no success. I asked whether he had also made representations to Hitler on 29 July, but Westphal said that this would have been useless, as Hitler regarded him as an 'Italophile'. The war diary of the German High Command gives the substance of the Field-Marshals' report to Hitler on that occasion without any reference to Operation Student.[58]

Westphal also expressed regret that Ambassador von Mackensen had lent himself to providing the list of General Student's prospective victims. He said that the Supreme Commander South and his staff would continue to try to prevent the operation, as it was not merely dishonourable and contrary to German military interests in Italy, but actually dangerous. But, in view of Hitler's only too well-known mentality, he had little hope that he would drop his planned revenge.

During the drive back to Rome I was in a highly agitated frame of mind. In the past few days I had certainly begun to count on grave German–Italian complications, on a possible breakdown of the alliance and sharp German counter-measures. But the idea of

[56] Ibid., p. 869.   [57] Ibid., p. 847.   [58] Ibid., p. 855.

pouncing treacherously and insidiously by night on the whole government of an allied nation in the middle of a war seemed to me to be so appalling that it put in the shade the worst stories of medieval banditry, because of the scale of the proposed *coup* and its inevitable repercussions, apart from anything else. There was no political or moral excuse for it. As we shall make clear later, at this time the Badoglio government had made no contact with the allies with a view to extricating Italy from the war. Nor was there any military excuse. On the contrary, Kesselring, the military commander-in-chief in the area, and Westphal, his Chief of Staff, who was well known for the quality of his military appreciations, as well as General von Rintelen, of course, and to a less extent Grand Admiral Doenitz and General Jodl, saw in it nothing but military disadvantages. Hitler's sole motive was the desire for political and personal revenge against men who had tried to free their country from the shackles of an ideology that it did not want or no longer wanted and had done it nothing but harm.

We were particularly dismayed by the extent to which the German reputation and German honour would be besmirched by this diabolical project. The German reputation had already been sufficiently damaged in other respects, not least by what had happened in the occupied territories. It was to be feared that such an assault on Rome would not be forgiven or forgotten, but would remain in the world's memory and survive in history books for a long time. The mere fact of a royal family being dragged down into the dust in such a treacherous manner by its own ally would cause the affair to be remembered with a shudder for generations.

A modern St. Bartholomew's Night in Rome would probably have been as harmful to the German reputation throughout the world as the 'Crystal Night' of 1938.

On the way back to Rome, under the depressing impact of the conference at Frascati, I yielded to the temptation of the most renegade thoughts. I remember Schiller's lines echoing in my ear, about one's beloved country, to which one should adhere, because that was where the roots of strength lay. I realized these words now faced me with a severe test. I was young, just thirty-one, the product of a Prussian family and a strict classical schooling and I had also been influenced by the principles and ways of thought of the German General Staff, and thus I was totally

unprepared to grapple with a situation in which there had been a complete reversal of values by the present rulers of Germany. My dislike of them had steadily increased and long since turned into loathing. On that 31 July it was tempting to draw the last bitter consequence, that is, to decide to join my Italian friends if it came to a final breach. I had in fact already discussed this possibility at home.

General von Rintelen did not return from his conversations at the Comando Supremo until late in the afternoon, and had hurriedly to prepare a full report of his negotiations with the Italian generals, so for the moment I was able to give him only a brief *résumé* of the Frascati meeting. But, as often happened, it was arranged that I should call on him at his home in the evening.

At this point, let me give some details about the planning of Operation Student, as well as the part played by the Embassy in the preparations up to 31 July.

On 25 July, after Hitler had heard about the change of government in Rome, he flew into a towering rage and expressed himself as follows at the 9.30 p.m. conference: 'But we'll do everything to grab the whole lot, clear out the whole gang. Tomorrow I'll send a man to order the Commander of the 3rd Panzer Grenadier Division to go into Rome with a special party to arrest the whole government, the King, the whole crew, and in particular arrest the Crown Prince at once and seize the whole rabble, particularly Badoglio and the whole gang. Then you'll see they'll tremble right down to their knees, and in two or three days there'll be another political upheaval.'[59] The reports of Hitler's conferences are very well worth reading and include many other examples of his way of speaking, which his colleagues had to listen to and put up with. He often addressed field-marshals and generals merely by their names or in the disrespectful second person when he was addressing a number of them.

At a conference in the early hours of the morning of 26 July Hitler was asked whether the exits of the Vatican should be occupied during the planned operations in Rome. His reply was: 'That's a matter of complete indifference to me, I'll go straight into the Vatican. Do you think I care about the Vatican? We'll grab it straight away. The chief thing about it is that the whole of the diplomatic corps are inside it. I don't give a damn. The whole

[59] Lage, p. 316.

gang are there, and we'll clear them all out. Then we can apologise afterwards, there's no need to worry about that.'[60] At another conference at 11.45 p.m. on the same day, when Badoglio was mentioned he said: 'If only I catch that pig.'[61]

A personal telegram to Mackensen on 26 July said: 'For reasons of principle we shall be interested in receiving the names of about thirty important personalities in the army, politics, and the royal family known to be notorious opponents of ours. Reich Foreign Minister requests your reply by secret cipher tonight.'[62]

Mackensen supplied the names of Ciano, Grandi, Volpi, Cerutti, and Suvich. In a later telegram he added that of Princess Isabella Colonna. He undertook to send a list of military personalities as soon as General von Rintelen had been consulted.

He pointed out, however, that the term 'notorious opponent' was very hard to interpret. He said that at all events no members of the royal family were to be regarded as 'notorious opponents'.[63]

After renewed pressure by the Foreign Ministry to produce a list of enemies of Germany in the Italian army, the following telegram was sent from Rome at midnight on 27 July: 'Military Attaché reports to me as follows on question of important army personalities known to us as notorious opponents: "There is no evidence that individual leading personalities in the Italian army can be described as definite enemies of the German Reich. In the Italian officers' corps rigid discipline and alignment with royal family prevails in attitude to allies or enemies. Also Fascism did not tolerate definitely anti-German elements among senior commanders. Any friction in military co-operation has been attributable, so far as we are aware, not to any basically hostile attitude but to divergent objective considerations or exaggerated sense of prestige. Nevertheless it is a fact that as a result of military events of the past year confidence in and admiration for the German army has generally declined, though that is not particularly striking among any definite Italian personalities." Mackensen.'[64]

Anyone who lived through that time of unbridled tyranny, or can imagine what it was like, will realize what a shining example of the then largely lost virtue of civil courage was displayed in this message by the German Military Attaché who, for the security

[60] Ibid., p. 329.   [61] Ibid., p. 349.
[62] A.A. Pol. Arch., Italien, Vol. 14, No. 72486.   [63] Ibid., No. 72495.
[64] Ibid., No. 72519.

reasons that we mentioned, could consult none of his colleagues before drafting it. He courageously defied his orders in every sentence of his message, and in particular, in his reference to the royal family that Hitler detested. He had been specifically ordered immediately to supply a list of names, and refused, because it would have imperilled the innocent. The tactically astute remark that the Fascists would not have tolerated anti-German elements in the top flight of generals must have been embarrassing to the recipients of this telegram.

Another example of loyalty to principles was also set on this occasion. A few days later Ambassador von Mackensen instructed the German consulates-general and consulates in Italy to supply the names of 'notorious opponents' of Germany, and Consul General von Halem sent a telegram from Milan that described the state of affairs succinctly and accurately: 'Wide circles in industry and aristocracy have always been Anglophile in attitude without this having led in practice to anti-German activity. The agents of anti-German propaganda are the anonymous masses. Hence for the time being the desired list cannot be supplied.'[65]

In view of Rintelen's refusal wrongly to describe anyone as guilty or suspect, the German leadership systematically entered the senior commanders of the Italian armed forces in General Student's list.

A final effort

Before going to General von Rintelen's flat on the evening of 31 July I had been turning over in my mind whether, in view of what was at stake, Rintelen should not make a last attempt to prevent the carrying out of Operation Student by making personal representations at headquarters, perhaps to Hitler himself. I was very well aware of the implications; he would be risking both his job and himself. Suggesting such a hazard to my immediate superior whom I respected so highly was a painful experience.

After a few sentences he interrupted and said he had already considered the idea that afternoon. But it was practically certain that any intervention coming from him would be useless. He had suggested coming to terms with the Italians only too often, with the result that his credit with Hitler and the High Command was

[65] Ibid., Vol. 15, No. 72757.

now too low for him to be able to hope to get anywhere in the face
of such fanatical decision. A long discussion followed, in which we
weighed up the pros and cons. I argued more and more keenly in
favour of making this last attempt in spite of its hazards, so that it
should be impossible to say later that we in Rome had left anything undone to bring the case for moderation and reason to
Hitler's personal attention.

At 11 p.m. von Rintelen secured Field-Marshal Keitel's telephoned consent to his making personal representations at headquarters.

The heat that night was tropical. Rintelen talked of the situation with great bitterness. The plan to strike at his long-standing
Italian friends hurt him deeply. Should he be instructed to take
a personal part in any action against Badoglio or Ambrosio, he
was determined to refuse to obey orders and accept the consequences.

Later inspection of the files has shown that Colonel Schuchardt,
the head of the attaché section at the Army General Staff, at about
the same time suggested to General Zeitzler, the Chief of the Army
General Staff, without previous consultation with Rome, that
General von Rintelen should be ordered to report to Hitler.
Schuchardt proposed that, in view of the apparently unfavourable
reception given to Field-Marshal Kesselring's representations to
Hitler on 29 July, another attempt should be made to influence
him by Rintelen. General Zeitzler thought that 'a completely
rigid view of things in Italy prevailed at the High Command', but
decided to think it over.[66]

Next morning—Sunday, 1 August—when he first got in touch
with the Comando Supremo, Rintelen told them that he was
going to fly to German headquarters. Soon afterwards they called
him back. Marshal Badoglio wished to talk to him before he left,
and asked him to call on him that afternoon at his villa in the Via
Bruxelles. His flight to Germany was therefore postponed to 2
August.

On the morning of 1 August Police Attaché Kappler gave me
the information he had promised about his interview with Himmler. The latter had shown him the ambassador's and the Military
Attaché's reports, and he had then been asked to state his objections to the German plans. He had said that he agreed entirely

[66] MGFA DZ, Akte H 27/57, No. 35.

with the views of the Military Attaché. Himmler had in many respects shown understanding, but had eventually got up and said: 'All this may be right or wrong. If there are perhaps many things that you do not understand today, then I must tell you that in this matter higher considerations prevail. The purposes and intentions of the National Socialist German Government therefore remain unchanged.' Kappler had thereupon assured Himmler of his unquestioning obedience.

The 'higher considerations' were obviously ideological. The Nazis refused to accept the downfall of Fascism, which both inside and outside the German frontiers threatened to bring about a dangerous increase in scepticism about the ability of the new ideas and methods to endure for the promised 1,000 years.

Kappler said that after this decision by his superior officer he withdrew his doubts and would devote all his energies to carrying out his orders. He again expressed regret that Dollmann had strengthened the mistaken views that had been formed in Germany in the past few days about political conditions in Italy. But at any rate his, Kappler's, conscience was clear, because he had stated his views without reference to the wishes of his superiors.

Finally he told me that after his return from Germany he had noted with astonishment how perceptive the Italians in Rome had become. They created the impression of knowing all about the plans for Operation Student. When I asked him where he suspected there might have been a leak, he contemptuously described the folly of the behaviour of German reconnaissance parties during the past few days in Rome. Dressed half in uniform, half in civilian clothes, members of the Skorzeny task force had kept driving past key-points in the city, in German army vehicles or on motor-cycles. In particular, they had cruised round the Villa Savoia with special frequency in this way. In any case, the Italians had received plenty of other indications to put them on their guard. Kappler knew nothing about any rumours from the Vatican.

Field-Marshal Kesselring followed up what General Student had been told at Frascati on 31 July about the rousing of Italian suspicions by a confirmatory telegram to the German High Command on 1 August in which he said that, while driving to the Comando Supremo that day, he himself had noted the strengthening of the security precautions and the guard. He had been forced to conclude that the Vatican rumour that the Germans were

planning a *coup* had led to tangible reactions. Surprise was no longer possible.[67]

Freiherr von Weizsäcker, the German Ambassador to the Holy See, telegraphed to Berlin at the same time: 'Several of my foreign diplomatic colleagues were given the following information yesterday evening: the Vatican believes itself to have definite evidence that a German military operation against Rome will take place in the next few days, for the purpose, among other things, of overthrowing the Badoglio government. The reason for this proposed action is said to be dissension between the German and Italian commands. When this was mentioned to me, I of course described it as imagination. I could not be sure my denial was believed.'[68]

The extent of Italian alarm is shown by entries in General Puntoni's diary. On 28 July he wrote: 'In the afternoon fears of a German reaction grew stronger. His Majesty gave me instructions to make all preparations for a possible departure from Rome. The King says: "I shall not risk undergoing the fate of the King of the Belgians. I want to be able to go on exercising the functions of head of state and to be able to decide in absolute freedom according to my own will." '

In an entry covering 1 and 2 August Puntoni wrote: 'The Villa Savoia has been put into a state of defence in order to prevent surprise. To increase their security I shall propose to their Majesties that they should move to the Quirinal, which is easier to defend against attack.'[69]

The important conversation between Badoglio and Rintelen before the latter's flight to headquarters took place at 4 p.m. on 1 August. The most important extracts of what the Marshal said are as follows:

I have sent for you as an old colleague whom I have known for seven years, to whom I can unburden myself as one soldier to another, as one friend to another.

The Fascist government collapsed of itself. The Fascist Grand Council passed a resolution against its own chief and brought it to the King's notice. The latter sent for Mussolini and said to him: 'You have lost, not only the confidence of the nation, but also that of your own party'. Mussolini thereupon asked to be relieved of office, to which the King agreed.

[67] Ktb. OKW, p. 875.   [68] A.A. Pol. Arch., Italien, Vol. 15, No. 72727.
[69] Puntoni, pp. 147 and 149.

Up to that point I was not involved. On Sunday, 25 July, at 5 p.m. I was informed by the Minister of the Royal Household, Acquarone, that I was to be received in audience by the King, who offered me the appointment of head of the government. To me this was like a blow on the head. At the age of seventy-two my only desire is to spend the evening of my life in peace and quiet. But as an old soldier I have to obey the call of my King.

After I had accepted, the King and I discussed the proclamation, the key phrase in which is: 'The war continues.' That was the assumption on which I accepted office. If the King had wished to capitulate, he would not have chosen a Marshal to be Prime Minister.

On Wednesday, the 28th, I sent a telegram to the Führer and proposed through General Marras that a meeting should take place at Treviso between the Führer and the King or me. The Führer declined, on the ground that the meeting at Feltre had recently taken place and that he was not available for the time being. He suggested a meeting of the Foreign Ministers of the two countries in which Keitel and Ambrosio should also take part. It will be necessary in this connection to examine the by no means simple situation frankly and openly and to tell us how far Germany can help us.

If the suspicion has arisen that we wish to make contact with the enemy with a view to making a separate peace, today's radio statement by Eisenhower has shown that we have not done this.

If this government falls, its place will be taken by a Bolshevik government. That is neither in our interests nor in yours.

If the German government believes it can get rid of the King and me, it will find out what 45 million easily excitable southerners can do.

If the Germans believe they can take over the government of this country, they will find out how difficult it is.

If I am to continue this war, I need the confidence of my ally. If we do not work together, the outcome will be bad for us both.

The situation is very grave. Large parts of the Italian army are outside the country. The enemy's supremacy is very great, especially in the air. Enemy production amounts to 9,500 aircraft a month, that of the Axis to only about 3,000.

The air raid on Rome, and even more the recent raids on Hamburg, have impressively demonstrated that superiority. Nevertheless Germany and Italy must stand together in order to bring about an early and honourable end to the war. If we fail to do this, there will be chaos in Europe.

Domestic political events in Italy are exclusively an Italian concern. They must not be allowed to influence relations between allies.

I have made this request that there should be confidence in the new

government, not to Ambassador von Mackensen, but to you as my old friend, because as a soldier I prefer talking to another soldier.

Help us to restore the mutual trust that is necessary to bring the war to an honourable conclusion.[70]

Rintelen and Montezemolo arranged to meet on the evening of 1 August, and I was drawn in. This long three-sided conversation in Rintelen's house confirmed Marshal Badoglio's statement that the Italian government hoped for German understanding of the necessity of jointly bringing the war to an early end. Montezemolo revealed his anxiety lest, as a result of German hostility, Italy might inevitably be forced into a position of disastrous isolation between Germany and the allies. He said that it was only by remaining together that Germany and Italy could obtain tolerable conditions for ending the war.

He again insisted, as he had done four days before at my flat, that the Italian government regarded the restoration of normal contact between the two governments as urgently necessary.

All statements by Italians in positions of authority on that and previous days led to the conclusion that they wanted a rapid normalization of relations with Germany, for three reasons:

In the first place, nothing must be left undone to reach an agreement with the German government on a solution that would spare the country from total ruin. This assumed—only too wrongly and optimistically—that the German government realized that the war must be ended before Germany's strength too was exhausted. Secondly, should Germany stubbornly insist on sacrificing Italy for the sake of prolonging her own defence, time must be gained for Italy to take steps to extricate herself from the alliance. Thirdly, the threat of violent German measures against the Italian government and armed forces must be averted by the resumption of normal relations.

The accompaniment to this conversation with Montezemolo on the evening of 1 August was the continual ringing of the telephone. Every call was concerned with recriminations between the German High Command and the Italian military authorities.

General Warlimont had telephoned several times during the day asking for immediate Italian consent to the entry into Italy of more German contingents. In the evening the Italians complained about high-handed behaviour by German troops in north Italy.

[70] Rintelen, pp. 229–32.

To prevent General von Rintelen from being interrupted too often in his conversation with Montezemolo, I had three times to accept inquiries by General De Stefanis, the Deputy Chief of the Italian Army General Staff, who wanted to know the meaning of the movements of German tanks that had been reported to him in the neighbourhood of his headquarters at Monterotondo, near Rome.

Telephone inquiries had to be made of all the German units that could possibly be involved before General De Stefanis could be given a reassuring answer. Also at the request of the German High Command, on the same night we had to secure withdrawal of the cancellation of troop movements in the Bolzano sector that had been ordered by the Comando Supremo because of the strain on the railway system.[71] Montezemolo shook his head at seeing this demonstration on our side of the fence of cross-fire between allies that caused the real enemy to be almost forgotten because of their mutual suspicions.

I drove Montezemolo home at about midnight. A few hundred yards from his home he asked me to stop; because of the gloomy thoughts racing through his head he wanted to walk the remaining distance. When we said good-bye he made another, almost desperate, appeal for confidence in Badoglio. He said that there was enough good will for a joint solution, but no more difficulties must be put in his government's way, thus driving it into isolation. He very much hoped that Rintelen would succeed in his mission next day. But, should things come to the pass of a German–Italian catastrophe, General von Rintelen and I could rely on Italian friendship and aid if we got into difficulties and needed such aid. Then he told me there was no need for me to reply and quickly got out of the car.

Next morning I accompanied Rintelen to the Ciampino North airfield. The special aircraft put at his disposal by the staff of the Supreme Commander South also carried Kesselring's usual greeting to Hitler, a big basket of fruit.

That morning a long conversation took place between Colonel-General Ambrosio and Field-Marshal Kesselring which I attended in Rintelen's absence. Again the chief topic was the arrival in Italy of German troops. Ambrosio again protested that these German contingents had not been given destinations in central or southern

[71] Ktb. OKW, p. 875.

Italy, but were to remain in north Italy in circumstances that created suspicion. Kesselring very patiently played down the alleged myth of a threat in northern Italy and, to pacify Ambrosio, remarked that it was to be expected that troop movements in a more southerly direction would take place soon. Ambrosio seemed tired of the everlasting squabbling and, in spite of the strain on the railway system, agreed in principle to the admission to Upper Italy of the 76th Infantry Division and one or two of the previously announced armoured divisions.[72] He made it a condition, however, that details of troop movements and quartering arrangements should first be agreed with the Italian Army General Staff.

This led to a conversation at 7.15 p.m. on the same day between Field-Marshal Kesselring and General Roatta at the War Ministry in the Via Venti Settembre, to which I accompanied the Field-Marshal. No one else was present. Roatta, wearing civilian clothes, spoke German almost exclusively. He began by being very accommodating in regard to the movements of the infantry units, and in our presence he immediately passed on our wishes by telephone to General di Raimondo, the head of Italian military transport. In his quick, nimble manner he also asked Raimondo to explain the transport situation, in case Kesselring should find the support given by the Italian railways insufficient in any respects. But no agreement was reached on the destination of the Leibstandarte Adolf Hitler and other armoured units that had been announced.

Roatta very frankly criticized the deployment of German troops in Italy. He said that the number of divisions, whether complete or represented by strong contingents, that had either arrived in Italy since the change of government or had been announced would soon amount to fourteen. Bearing in mind the urgent Italian requests for reinforcements in June and July, this aid, which had been refused out of hand and declared to be impossible at the time, but had now been provided with such surprising speed, should now really be greeted with great pleasure and gratitude. Unfortunately, however, all hopes and plans had been thrown into confusion by the fact that these troops, contrary to all military reason, were being kept in the back areas in Upper Italy. Or—he must once more quite frankly ask—were there secret German intentions in regard to the employment of these troops? At all events, in his responsible position as Chief of the Army General

[72] Ibid., p. 881.

Staff he could not conceal from his ally the view that this German behaviour made the prospects of a successful continuation of the war against the British and the Americans extremely slender.

Field-Marshal Kesselring repeated what he had said to Colonel-General Ambrosio in the morning. It was necessary to be patient and to wait a little longer. In many cases the German troops' destination was certainly only provisional. The question whether the enemy intended to invade the northern half of the Italian boot had to be cleared up first. Also the railway system did not allow so many troops to be transported to the south immediately. Roatta vigorously disputed this. He said that transport difficulties on a substantial scale existed only in the frontier area and in Upper Italy. In any case, a large proportion of these troops could be moved south by road if there was any intention of doing so.

The conversation ended with a very remarkable little exchange. Roatta remarked, quite nonchalantly and casually: 'Oh, Field-Marshal, I hear you have assembled two infantry regiments and a large number of parachute troops here near Rome, and in particular near Frascati. May I ask whether this is for any particular purpose?'

Kesselring cheerfully and spontaneously replied: 'I wanted to strengthen the defence of my headquarters against enemy landings from the air. Practically nothing had previously been done to ensure the security of my headquarters.'

Thereupon Roatta, with magnificently restrained cynicism, said: 'But, Field-Marshal, you have no need to worry, no one will ever do anything to you up there. Of course it can be said that it's always a good thing to be on the safe side. I too have just strengthened the security of my headquarters at Monterotondo.'

Thus the two allied commanders sat there like actors in a bandit play—the brigand-against-his-will making transparent statements and the intended victim hinting that he would defend himself. The code-word that would set Operation Student in motion might arrive at any moment.

That evening Prince Bismarck, Counsellor von Kessel of the German Embassy to the Holy See, and I were Doertenbach's guests. Nearly all the members of the diplomatic families had already left for Germany, partly for the summer holidays, to escape the heat in Rome, and partly because of the growing acuteness of the situation in Italy. At Doertenbach's there was a long

conversation certainly not meant for foreign ears. We spoke of the gravity of the situation and expressed indignation at the crimes of the government and the party both inside and outside Germany. It was intelligible that we should take refuge in thoughts of a better future when, after the inevitable military defeat, it would be possible to build again on new foundations such as those the Italians were trying to establish before our eyes. In thinking about these things we were certainly anticipating events by a long chalk, but it was comforting in that agitated situation to discuss between four walls the possible shape of a new Germany.

For security reasons General von Rintelen, in a brief telephone conversation from headquarters late that evening, could give no details about the outcome of his conversations, but I gathered from a hint that a final decision on Operation Student had not yet been made, but that the possibility of at least a postponement was not excluded.

I spent the afternoon of 3 August at the Comando Supremo. First of all I had to submit a list of German requests and wishes to General Rossi and, after a number of other conversations, I was present at a talk between General Rossi and Major-General Westphal. There was a difference of view about Anglo-American intentions. Westphal did his utmost to defend the German High Command claim, which he did not believe in, that a threat to north Italy existed. Rossi roundly refused to accept this, and stoutly argued that the next allied objective could be only south and central Italy. Another thing discussed was the increasing difficulties being experienced in transporting German divisions from France, through the area of the Italian Fourth Army on the French Riviera. The Italian view was that the Germans were not allowing enough time for their requirements to be fulfilled; excessive demands were being put on the railway system and the quartering situation.

The conversation was conducted in a thoroughly polite, even friendly, manner. General Rossi concluded by expressing thanks for the German reinforcements that had now been made available in Italy. It was hard to detect to what extent the rather taciturn deputy chief of the Comando Supremo meant this ironically.

3 August also went by without Operation Student being set in motion.

As usually happens at times of crisis, fresh news tended as much

H

to confuse as to clarify the situation. An example of this was a telegram sent that day by Ambassador von Mackensen saying that Hidaka, the Japanese Ambassador in Rome, had urgently recommended the establishment of friendly relations with the Italian government, as Badoglio definitely intended to continue the war.[73] On the other hand, according to a note by State Secretary von Steengracht on 4 August, Oshima, the Japanese Ambassador in Berlin, expressed the opinion that the Italians were already negotiating with the allies. Oshima therefore suggested that a watch be kept on the Italian fleet by German dive-bombers.[74]

General von Rintelen flew back to Rome on the afternoon of 4 August. It had been feared that Hitler would make him pay for his presumption in making personal representations about the situation in Italy by not allowing him to return to his post. His recall, however, occurred only several weeks later.

At headquarters on 2 August he had had an unpleasant surprise. On the way to the interview with Hitler Field-Marshal Keitel had whispered to him that in no circumstances should he mention Operation Student; the Führer must not be allowed to know that he had any knowledge of it. In view of his order that the number of those initiated must be kept to an absolute minimum, he would burst into a rage if he discovered that Rintelen was in the know. This hint, which had to be regarded as an order, made Rintelen's task much more difficult. He had flown to headquarters specifically to state the objections to the operation and point out the catastrophic consequences that would ensue. But now in the decisive interview he would have to bury it in an account of the general situation in Italy and his last conversation with Badoglio. Thus he could only indirectly indicate to Hitler how misguided and dangerous the project was.

Hitler's mood, as expected, was a mixture of anger, wounded pride, vengefulness, and strong suspicion of the new Italian government. He was still convinced that it had long since put out feelers towards the allies. But he thought it possible that such feelers had met with an unsatisfactory response, and that Badoglio wanted better relations with Germany for that reason. Nevertheless Rintelen succeeded in getting Hitler to listen and even to reconsider the situation. He did not reject out of hand the idea that it was in the German interest to re-establish normal co-operation

[73] A.A. Pol. Arch., Italien, Vol. 15, No. 72764.   [74] Ibid., No. 72802.

with the Comando Supremo, at any rate for the time being; this, in fact, bore fruit in the preparations for the meeting at Tarvisio that had meanwhile been arranged. The Foreign Ministers and military leaders were to meet there soon for a first exchange of views since the upheaval in Italy.

It reflects the greatest credit on Rintelen's efforts that, in spite of the unfavourable prospects and the hostility he inevitably met with, his interview with Hitler on 2 August led to the postponement of Operation Student. The result of the postponement was that Hitler ended by finally dropping it in the course of the month. According to the record of Hitler's conferences, 'after Rintelen submitted Badoglio's assurances of fidelity on 2 August, Hitler became more conciliatory and stopped Operation Student, which subsequently was never carried out'.[75]

General Westphal states in his memoirs that Kesselring's and Rintelen's adroitness prevented Hitler from carrying out his intention of using armed force against Rome, and thereby did a service to the German reputation.[76] This brief phrase does not do sufficient justice to that service. It prevented an appalling crime. Kesselring's written objections had not made Hitler change his mind, but Rintelen, apart from the skill and patience he showed in his interview with the Führer, had the luck that often plays a part in success; he was in the right place at the right time.

A few days later the Army General Staff, Section Foreign Armies West, submitted a full and very realistic appreciation that among other things advised against a *coup* against Badoglio, and after 2 August Kesselring again expressed himself in the same sense. These documents were, however, submitted to the Army General Staff only on 2 and 8 August,[77] and it is not known when Hitler saw them. Their value lay in the fact that they provided further backing for Hitler's decision to postpone the operation after Rintelen's interview with him. But for the latter's intervention, they would have been too late to influence it. The dates foreseen for Operation Student were 2, 3, or 4 August, as General Student repeatedly declared in the course of the conference at Frascati on 31 July.

[75] Lage, p. 316.
[76] Siegfried Westphal, *Heer in Fesseln*, Frankfurt and Bad Godesberg, 1950, p. 224.
[77] Ktb. OKW, p. 896 f.

It has subsequently been sometimes suggested that on 2 August Rintelen gave Hitler a wrong assessment of the situation, his pro-Italian attitude having a misled him into accepting as genuine Badoglio's assurance about joint continuation of the war.

Light was thrown on this question by Mario Badoglio, the Marshal's son and close colleague, at a full discussion with General von Rintelen in 1952. He said that the idea of dissociating himself from an ally in wartime had weighed heavily on his father's conscience. It was easier for his civilian advisers to consider it than it was for a soldier who after fifty-four years' service had reached the highest rank his country had to offer. He had therefore clung to the hope that a way might be found of bringing the war to an end in the foreseeable future in co-operation with Germany and in agreement with the German leadership.

In order to work towards this a continuation of the joint struggle was obviously desirable for the time being. Mario Badoglio said that for this reason his father had had high hopes that Rintelen's mission to Hitler would open the way to frank discussions. The aged Marshal had many times confirmed this after the war.[78]

It must further be pointed out, in regard to Rintelen's interview with Hitler, that his primary purpose was to prevent the carrying out of Operation Student. Had Rintelen expressed any doubt about Badoglio's loyalty to the alliance, his mission would have been condemned to failure from the outset, and there would have been no point in running the risk involved. 'Higher considerations' were at stake, though these were of a different nature from those of Hitler, Himmler, or Göring. The purpose was to prevent an intolerable stain on German honour and stop a militarily useless step from being taken. Hence he was forced on 2 August to stake everything on a single card.

His own doubts at the time were concentrated on the question of when the King and Badoglio, because of the unapproachable and threatening behaviour of the Germans, would give up trying to find a solution jointly with them.

On 2 August there was no concrete evidence that they had done so. In this situation not only Rintelen, but a number of other clear-

[78] Personal communication from General von Rintelen on this conversation with Mario Badoglio.

sighted representatives of the Army General Staff took care not to pour oil on the flames of Hitler's suspicions, which would have only increased the danger of precipitate action.

General von Rintelen repeated Badoglio's statement of 1 August as far as possible in the Marshal's own words. He mentioned Badoglio's assurance that his appointment as head of the government had come to him as a complete surprise. An attempt is made in the war diary of the German High Command to cast doubt on Badoglio's veracity in this matter.[79] It claims that this statement was later refuted by information given in the newspaper *Lavoro Fascista* of the end of September 1943. According to this, Badoglio and Grandi were received by the King before 25 July to make preparations for a *coup d'état*. It is sufficient to read Deakin's thorough investigation of the prehistory of 25 July to appreciate that, let alone their being received together by the King, there was no contact between Grandi and Badoglio at that time.

The war diary of the High Command also states that the speed with which the acute crisis of 25 July was dealt with shows that it must have been preceded by careful secret preparations. That too is a false conclusion. Seldom in history has the overthrow of a government been more overdue and less prepared for than that of 25 July 1943 in Italy.[80]

It is difficult to understand why a statement in a party newspaper was accepted as evidence by the war diary of the German High Command. The *Lavoro Fascista* was one of the first daily newspapers to appear after the setting up of the neo-Fascist rump republic in Upper Italy at the end of September 1943. As was to be expected, it began by conducting a violent propaganda campaign against the monarchy and the Badoglio government, and it daily distorted all the events that led to Mussolini's downfall. The war diary of the German High Command should never have drawn on such a source. In February 1944, when I was questioned about events in Italy at the Army General Staff, I was shown this copy of the *Lavoro Fascista* and I strongly recommended that it should be ignored as unreliable.

---

[79] Ktb. OKW, p. 830 f.

[80] This is confirmed by the latest Italian historiography so far as the meeting of the Fascist Grand Council that led to Mussolini's fall is concerned.

There is, however, one statement made to Rintelen by Marshal Badoglio on 1 August, namely that his call to office was like 'a blow on the head', that deserves a moment's consideration.

It did not come to him completely as a bolt from the blue. For one thing, the King had received him on 15 July, the date on which he, Caviglia, and Thaon De Revel were 'short listed' as possible successors to Mussolini in the event of his sudden fall. For another, he was very well aware in July 1943 that things were coming to a head in Italy, though he could not know what was going to happen, or how. Nevertheless it was a great shock to him when he was informed at the last moment by Acquarone that the choice had fallen on him. Though the possibility had been secretly discussed for some days, a man of seventy-two had the right to say that when he was confronted with the fact of his appointment as head of the government it came to him like a 'blow on the head'.

The meagreness of the preparations made for the change of government is also shown by the choice and first appearance of the new Italian Foreign Minister. Raffaele Guariglia was Italian Ambassador in Ankara. He was informed of his appointment on 26 July by telephone via Budapest, and he succeeded in arriving in Rome to take up his appointment only on 29 July. A number of protocol difficulties, including the making of the first contacts with the Germans, arose from the fact that the Badoglio government did not have a Foreign Minister available from the outset. If Mussolini's overthrow had been planned, as the German High Command war diary and the propaganda of the neo-Fascist régime in Upper Italy claimed, a Foreign Minister would certainly have been chosen in advance and would have taken over immediately. If the change of government had been planned, this would have been treated as a matter of special urgency in view of the political and military situation of Italy in July 1943 and her relations with Germany.

Shortly before General von Rintelen returned from his trip to Germany on 4 August the following communication from the Comando Supremo landed on his desk, illustrating the continuing Italian–German tension in north Italy:

'On 31 July,' it said, 'German units on the march near Colle Sacro (Bolzano) called out: "Long Live Rome, we are going to free the Duce." Rumour has it that two motorized or armoured divisions are to proceed to Milan and Rome to free the Duce.

Your Excellency will not fail to note the extraordinary delicate nature of this communication, or the absolute necessity of German troops' refraining from any utterances on Italian domestic questions. It is requested that the above shall be communicated to the German High Command. (Signed) Ambrosio.'[81]

[81] MGFA DZ, Akte W o 1–7/286, Militär-Attaché Rom, 1a No. 2775/43, Geheime Kommandosache, 4.8.1943.

III

The Alliance Falls Apart

Soon after the German rejection of the proposal by the King and Marshal Badoglio that there should be a meeting between the German and Italian heads of State, it became known at the German Embassy in Rome that Hitler and Ribbentrop were suggesting that if the meeting took place on Italian soil the Italians would arrest the German leaders. We also knew that the Italians suspected that the King and Badoglio might never return from conversations in Germany.

Hitler's and Ribbentrop's suspicions were totally unfounded, while those of the Italians were only too well justified.

The Italians would never have dared take such action against Hitler and his entourage. They were only too well aware that the relations of strength between the Germans and Italians in Italy made the idea totally inconceivable. The German army dominated the whole of Italy. Most of the Italian divisions were outside the country, and the forces at home were so weak that they could easily have been disarmed by a German military *coup*.

If the King and his senior civilian and military advisers had gone to a meeting in Germany, the picture would have been very different. If they had been arrested, Italy would have been unable to lift a finger. The Italian government had good reason to believe that the idea had been discussed in Germany. In unofficial approaches from the German side it had been only too often suggested, for instance, that the Crown Prince should take part in top-level conversations, should these take place. Ambassador von Mackensen was instructed to press the suggestion in a conversation with Foreign Minister Guariglia on 1 August.[1] Apart from the suspected German intention of arresting him too, to prevent him from stepping into his father's shoes, the Italians could see no good reason for involving him.

On 1 August Badoglio said openly to Rintelen that the German government was suspected of planning to get rid of the King and

[1] A.A. Pol. Arch., Italien, Vol. 15, No. 72705.

him. Mario Pansa, the Deputy Chief of Protocol in the Italian Foreign Ministry, said to Prince Bismarck on 3 August that the rumour that the Germans were going to arrest the King 'was in the air'. Montezemolo told me on 3 and 4 August that the Italians had very definite information about 'remarkable German intentions'. He added, out of politeness, that he nevertheless assumed that these were not to be taken seriously, but were merely nervous and precipitate reactions to the first surprise after 25 July.

On 3 and 4 August preparations for the conversations between the Foreign Ministers and between Field-Marshal Keitel and Colonel-General Ambrosio were intensified. It was eventually arranged that they should take place on 6 August at Tarvisio, on the German–Italian frontier.

The situation on 3 August as seen from Rome is summarized by four telegrams sent that day. First of all, Colonel von Veltheim, the German Deputy Air Attaché, reported from apparently reliable sources the following statements made by the Crown Prince's civilian *chef de cabinet*: 'Italy is militarily completely done for. It is feared that even German aid will no longer be sufficient to save her. There is no intention of putting out peace feelers. The possibility of peace for Italy depends on the Führer. It is secretly hoped that he will appreciate the Italian predicament. But even if he takes a different view, the royal family will abide by its treaty obligations.' It turned out later that this statement made in circles close to the Crown Prince was explained by the fact that the latter was deliberately kept away from all questions of the day and urgent political problems by the King and Badoglio and was left exclusively to the command of his army group.

A telegram from Rintelen on the same day said: 'Marshal Badoglio said to a close friend that he was determined to continue the war to a common end and was surprised that the Germans had no confidence in him. His declaration that the war would continue had made him millions of enemies in his own country. If Italy and Germany did not keep together and failed to grapple jointly with the difficult situation, he foresaw one of the greatest calamities of all time for Europe.'

Rintelen further said that, in accordance with instructions, he had informed Badoglio that the reason for the presence of German reinforcements in Upper Italy was the danger of allied landings and the possibility of internal unrest in Italy. Badoglio had replied

that Communist unrest had been firmly suppressed by his government within two days. This was purely an Italian domestic affair,
and all was now quiet. But the entry of German troops had been
like an advance into hostile territory. Doubts about the course his
government was taking were easily disposed of by reading the
foreign press, which was already severely criticizing him. He again
appealed for good German–Italian co-operation.

The fourth telegram, sent by Mackensen, said:

A veteran Fascist said Fascism had recently been too Nazi-oriented.
The party leaders had failed to recognise that the Italian people must
be treated differently from the German. Italian citizens must have a
feeling of actively participating in some way in the conduct of state
affairs. Instead Fascism had turned them into objects having no will or
initiative. That explained why the idea of liberty proclaimed by Badoglio had met with such a response from the Italian people and had caused
a thoroughly genuine sense of satisfaction. The Italian people were not
yet ripe for Fascism and totalitarianism on the Nazi model.[2]

Late in the afternoon of 5 August General von Rintelen left in a
special train with the Italian delegation to attend the meeting at
Tarvisio.

I spent the evening with Major Marchesi at a *trattoria* in the
centre of Rome, and we had a long and very frank talk. Marchesi
spoke of the way in which the authority of the Badoglio government was being shackled by the Germans. In the absence of calm
and factual discussion of the future conduct of the war and, above
all, of how it should be brought to an end as the situation required,
the position would become intolerable. It could not be assumed
that Italy wished to extricate herself from the war on her own
account, because that would certainly lead to the destruction of
the country by the Germans. Also Italy still lay under the odium
of not having kept her word to the Central Powers, Germany and
Austria, in 1915, and this had not been forgotten. On the contrary,
it was still a warning and an encumbrance in the eyes of responsible politicians. But Germany must not exploit the Italian predicament to drive Italy into taking a desperate step. Germany must
finally recognize what were the real prospects if the war
continued or in what way it could be brought to an end with as

[2] Ibid., Nos. 72806, 72810, 72811, and 72813.

little damage as possible. Next day's conversations at Tarvisio might well be the last chance for this.

Marchesi described in detail how gravely the present German attitude to Italy, which had now come to herself again, hampered the functioning of the government and the army command. All the essential conditions for future planning were lacking, and even the conferences at the Comando Supremo suffered in these circumstances. Ambrosio and Rossi were more reticent than usual. A veil of secrecy overlay everything, and it was to be hoped that it would be lifted at Tarvisio next day. Also the intolerable threat of a *colpo di forza* by the SS and parachute troops must be finally swept away.

On this last point, Marchesi asked whether I could give him an assurance that it could be regarded as finally buried. I replied that in many respects a veil of secrecy prevailed with us too. Of course we at the embassy were not blind to the conspicuous behaviour of certain German troops in and around Rome. The first shock caused by the upheaval of 25 July had led in many quarters to the exaggerated view that it was necessary to take steps to ensure the security of the German troops and offices that were scattered widely all over the peninsula. But I had the hope and also the impression that this excitement was now gradually yielding to a calmer frame of mind. However, as he had himself stated, we had certainly not yet overcome the stage of mutual suspicion.

The talk ended with a plea by Marchesi that a disaster should be prevented that could bring the Germans no benefit. The Comando Supremo was gratefully aware that General von Rintelen had such an excellent knowledge of conditions in Italy. In view of the fact that the German Ambassador had involuntarily put himself in a difficult and embarrassing position by his previous co-operation with the Fascists, the government highly appreciated the fact that it was possible to discuss everything with the Military Attaché. Recent developments has also caused difficulties for the Italian Embassy in Berlin. Ambassador Alfieri, who had voted for Grandi's resolution, i.e. against Mussolini, at the meeting of the Grand Council, was now in an impossible situation in Nazi Germany. A new ambassador would have to be appointed soon.

When we said goodnight that evening, Marchesi cautiously repeated the hint given to me by Montezemolo on the evening of 1 August. He said that situations could arise in life in which an identity of outlook between members of different nationalities

could have greater importance than loyalty to a system of government in one's own country that obviously did not give due place to the idea of liberty. This thought had often passed through his mind in the last phases of Mussolini's government, when Italy had been staggering with giant strides towards the edge of the abyss.

I was convinced that these hints of Montezemolo and Marchesi were not to be understood as an attempt to win Rintelen and me over to their side in order to have crown witnesses against Germany. At this time, as we shall show later, Italy's prospects of securing an armistice for herself were not nearly tangible enough. These hints were an expression of genuine friendship. At most it could be suggested that they were associated with the hope that we should intensify our efforts to prevent the planned violent measures and also, perhaps, warn our Italian friends about them in good time.

Hitler's instructions for the Tarvisio conversations on 6 August were that efforts should be concentrated on eliciting Italian intentions, and that Ribbentrop and Keitel should therefore leave most of the talking to the Italians. The German intention of evacuating Sicily must not be mentioned. This entry in the war diary of the German High Command sounds surprising.[3] In his appreciation of the situation dated 4 August Marshal Kesselring had stated with his usual optimism: 'The Sicilian bridgehead can continue to be held for some time if casualties are quickly replaced, sufficient ammunition is sent, and the air defence is strengthened.'[4] Thus he did not set unfulfillable conditions, but as usual underestimated the reinforcements on which the enemy could draw. Also he did not take sufficiently into account the battle-weary condition of the few German divisions in Sicily. But it is surprising that Hitler was thinking of giving up the struggle in Sicily before Kesselring was.

The order not to discuss the intention to evacuate the island with the Italians may have been a not unclever move in the short term, but it involved the danger that German over-all plans for the continuation of the war, which the Italians so desperately wanted to know, would again be withheld from them. This was bound to lead quickly to disharmony again.

It will appear later, in our account of the steps by which Italy went over to the allies, that the King, at Guariglia's instigation,

[3] Ktb. OKW, p. 900.   [4] Ibid., p. 896.

had given his consent to a first cautious approach to the allies several days before the meeting at Tarvisio.

It had been decided, under the impact of the German attitude after 25 July that, to provide for all eventualities in the further development of German–Italian relations, a first tentative approach to the other side should be made without any final commitment to that course.

It was feared that, if an irreparable breach with Germany took place and Italy had then to take the first difficult steps towards extricating herself from an untenable position, valuable time would have been lost which it would be impossible to make good.

Thus the policy that was adopted was double-pronged; to try and find a way out of the war for Italy in conjunction with Germany and, should this turn out to be impossible, to take steps with a view to acting independently. The Italians also wanted to find out as soon as possible what prospects there were of obtaining acceptable terms from the allies.

At Tarvisio the German delegation created a superfluously hostile atmosphere from the outset. Ribbentrop and Keitel arrived at the station in a heavily armoured train, which was then cordoned off by SS men—on Italian soil. In order to be conciliatory, the representatives of the Italian Foreign Ministry, instead of the civilian clothes that became usual again with the disappearance of Fascism, wore diplomatic uniform without Fascist emblems. They actually went so far as to greet the Germans with raised right arms, though to the great satisfaction of the great majority of the population the Fascist salute had been abolished in Italy after 25 July.

The Italian delegation was led by Guariglia. His reputation as a skilful negotiator was known to the Germans, who also knew his reactions in Ankara to the news of the collapse of Fascism and his appointment as Foreign Minister.

On 27 July Ambassador von Papen reported from the Turkish capital that Guariglia had said that the war must be continued, as Badoglio had announced, but that the aim of bringing it to an end by political means must simultaneously be pursued. He did not believe that Italy could hold out militarily for long. Germany, however, could obviously go on fighting, but in the long run would

be at a disadvantage. He summed up his programme as 'abandoning dreams and returning to reality'. He hoped for close co-operation with Berlin and for appreciation of the situation as it affected both countries alike. The relatively short period during which Italy would be able to hold out and maintain a negotiating position must be fully exploited.[5]

These were certainly over-hasty remarks that were bound to rouse German suspicions. The conversations at Tarvisio nevertheless did not result in an open breach. It can be claimed that Guariglia actually impressed Ribbentrop by his negotiating skill and the dexterity of his replies.

He began by insisting that the changes that had taken place in his country were an exclusively Italian affair. To doubt the statement made by two soldiers, the King and Marshal Badoglio, that the war would be continued would be a deep insult to Italian national pride and honour.

Ribbentrop tried to make the most of anti-German incidents that had taken place in which diplomats had been involved. By this he meant primarily the demonstration against the German Consulate General at Turin. That incident had been interpreted in Germany as a dangerous expression of popular opinion. Guariglia denied this; he pointed out that such events were inevitable in a big country at a time of political confusion when the masses were on the move. His government naturally greatly deplored the Turin incident, but it was a cause for satisfaction that more incidents had not occurred.

To Ribbentrop's question of how the new government visualized future developments, Guariglia replied as follows. As before, the allies in their public statements called for the unconditional surrender both of Italy and Germany. Hence the Italian people had no choice but to continue the war. By the realities of the situation of which he had spoken at Ankara he meant the war and the alliance with Germany. These realities also included—and here a very confused sentence follows—'the intentions of the enemy, who seek by peaceful means to obtain what they must conquer by force of arms'.

The Italian government had no 'special ideas' about the continuation of the war, and in particular none that departed from the attitude of the previous Italian government. Mussolini had

[5] A.A. Pol. Arch., Italien, Vol. 14, No. 72418.

several times expressed to Hitler his concern at the possibility that no solution might be found on the eastern front. He also recalled the earlier Italian proposal that public declarations should be made presenting the people of Europe with a convincing political vision for the future. This could be done only in co-operation between Germany and Italy. Also, after the loss of her colonial empire and as a consequence of the difficulties in the Balkans, Italy's prospects remained closely linked with Germany's in every other respect.

The German Foreign Minister asked whether any negotiations had taken place between Italy and the allies.

Guariglia gave him the Italian government's word that no negotiations had been begun.

He declared that a capitulation was impossible. One capitulated under enemy pressure, but there could be no question of a 'cold capitulation'. 'On capitule sous la pression de l'ennemi, mais on ne capitule pas à froid.' It was possible that irresponsible persons were carrying on negotiations about which he knew nothing.

Colonel-General Ambrosio, called on to speak about the military situation, said in broad outline that, so far as military co-operation was concerned, nothing had changed from the Italian point of view. It had caused surprise that so many German divisions had arrived in Italy unannounced. None of the German–Italian agreements covering the arrival and stationing of troops in Italy were being abided by. The deployment of German troops no longer accorded with Italian but only with German interests. In this connection he must specifically mention the concentration of German troops round Rome.

Field-Marshal Keitel, raising his voice, said that on the way to the airfield after the talks at Feltre on 19 July he had given Ambrosio a firm promise of four divisions and held out the prospect of two more.

Examination of all the available documents and memoirs of those concerned has so far produced no evidence to corroborate this statement.

A memorandum by the German Army General Staff dated 4 August 1943, drafted in preparation for the negotiations with the Comando Supremo at Tarvisio on 6 August, shows that no such promise was made at Feltre. It states that the intention was

announced at Feltre of sending further large contingents to southern Italy, two infantry divisions to begin with, but that it would not be possible to do this until the German forces in Sicily and southern Italy had been brought up to full strength and were assured of sufficient supplies for a long period.[6] Thus at Feltre two infantry divisions were promised in the long term, but no firm promise of four divisions was given, and the prospect of two more was not held out.

As we know, the Italians returned from Feltre in a state of gloom because they had obtained none of the binding German promises for which they had so ardently hoped for the defence of Sicily, where fighting had just begun. General Roatta makes this point very clearly in his memoirs and points out the consequences that ensued for the conduct of the struggle in Sicily and for German–Italian relations.[7]

We have gone into this incident in some detail because it illustrates how unobjectively and dictatorially the Italian ally was often treated, and how statements were often made that contradicted previous statements.

Ambrosio's statement at Tarvisio was followed by a long fencing match on whether German troops were in Italy to re-establish order in the sense in which the Germans interpreted the term or whether they were there to help at the front. Guariglia remarked that it was very intelligible that suspicion should arise in connection with the first point.

In a *tête-à-tête* with Ribbentrop, Guariglia gave him an assurance that the Badoglio government would permit the survival of many Fascist institutions, e.g. the syndicates, the corporations, and the Dopolavoro (recreational activities) organization, and would allow Fascists of unblemished character to remain in office. This was intended to reassure the Germans and also to divert them from other ticklish themes.

At the end of the conversation Ribbentrop, without mentioning any date or place, suggested a top-level meeting, to be attended by all the leading personalities from the King of Italy to the appropriate representatives of the Comando Supremo, and he added that the presence of Crown Prince Umberto was especially desired. He said that the possibility could not be excluded that the new

[6] MGFA DZ, Akte III W 57, Sheet 29.
[7] Mario Roatta, *Otto Milioni di Baionette*, Milan, 1946, pp. 274 and 283.

I

Italian government might one day be displaced just as suddenly as Mussolini had been displaced. This was not a very polite remark to the representatives of the Italian government in office. Guariglia briefly replied that Italy had herself suggested a top-level meeting many days ago.[8]

In his memoirs Rintelen sums up the results of the Tarvisio meeting as follows: 'The conversations did not yield any positive result. The mistrust dictated by Hitler no longer permitted frank discussion. No agreement on the purpose of continuing the struggle was reached. The Italians wanted to bring about an early end of the war, and the Germans refused all discussion of that subject. No attempt was made to hold firm or support the wavering ally. So Ambrosio and Guariglia returned from Tarvisio convinced that Italy must go her own way. Their plainly demonstrated rejection by the (German) political and military leadership morally facilitated their baling out.'[9]

Guariglia comments as follows in his book: 'When we said goodbye, the greetings we exchanged were less cool than they were on our arrival.' He regarded it as a success that he had succeeded in gaining a breathing-space. But, so he wrote in retrospect, the situation required that it be used without the loss of a moment for reaching the most necessary agreements with the allies.[10]

Ribbentrop instructed Ambassador von Mackensen not to return to Rome in the Italian special train, but to accompany him in his train to Germany. Mackensen never returned to his post in Rome. He was out of favour. During the weeks that followed Prince Bismarck acted as Chargé d'Affaires.

He had occasion to feel the burden of this office immediately after returning from Tarvisio. A lively dispute arose about the *communiqué* to be issued; misunderstandings and disagreements at first made it impossible to find a formula acceptable to both sides. The Germans claimed that a draft had been shown to the Italians at Tarvisio and approved by them, but the Italians disputed this when they were asked to agree to the proposed German version on the morning of 7 August.

Ribbentrop wanted the *communiqué* to emphasize that full agreement had been reached on measures for the future conduct of the

---

[8] A.A. Pol. Arch., Büro Reichsminister, Handakten Dolmetscher Schmidt, 1943, Part II, Nos. 48793–840.
[9] Rintelen, p. 238.   [10] Guariglia, p. 629 f.

war, while Badoglio wanted a brief statement that would not irritate the allies and above all would not give them an excuse for carrying out the massive air raids on Rome that were feared. Negotiations were in progress through the Vatican with a view to declaring Rome an open city. Badoglio asked Bismarck to secure German appreciation of the disastrous consequences that would follow a heavy bombing of Rome. Apart from the effect on morale in Italy, it would have a grave effect on the military transport situation and hence the defence of Sicily. Badoglio let it be seen that Guariglia had not sufficiently emphasized this point at Tarvisio.[11]

The Italian attitude in this tug-of-war over the *communiqué* undoubtedly displayed a striking regard for the allies. On the other hand, a heavy Anglo-American air strike at Rome would have been a severe blow to the new government, which was trying to gain time until either Rome was declared an open city or the most important government offices had been evacuated.

Badoglio took the tactical step of blaming Guariglia for not having drawn sufficient attention to these considerations at Tarvisio, and this became the Italian official line.

Dollmann, who promptly interfered here again, seized on this matter, as appears from a telegram dated 11 August from Kaltenbrunner, the chief of the security police, to the Foreign Ministry: 'In a conversation of Dollmann's with Castellano on the *communiqué* question Dollmann gained the impression of an increasing rejection of Guariglia by the generals.'[12] Castellano knew that Guariglia was being used as a scapegoat to divert the Germans from the heart of the problem. There was no question of any dissension between Guariglia and the leading generals. This was shown during the weeks that followed, when major joint decisions were made by the Badoglio government's civilian and military leaders.

Castellano incidentally states in his memoirs that in this conversation Dollmann threatened violent measures by the SS if differences with the Italian police arose.[13]

Between 7 and 9 August German–Italian friction reached its height in the Brenner frontier zone. General Feurstein, the German commander there, continually attempted by threats and

---

[11] A.A. Pol. Arch., Italien, Vol. 15, Nos. 72837–41.
[12] Ibid., No. 72906.   [13] Castellano, *L'armistizio*, p. 79 f.

ultimatory demands to eliminate the Italians from guarding the railway line from the Brenner to Bolzano. News reached Rome daily of incidents in which Germans and Italians nearly resorted to the use of arms. Colonel-General Ambrosio firmly pointed out that it had been agreed at Tarvisio that two weak Alpini divisions should carry out this task jointly with German troops, and in support of this he was able to quote the report of the Tarvisio conversations. The German High Command had obviously omitted to inform General Feurstein of this. The situation was aggravated by the fact that Hofer, the Gauleiter and Governor of Tyrol-Vorarlberg, intervened to make trouble. He expressed the suspicion that the Italian moves were the result of an Anglo-American stipulation that Italy would secure better peace terms if she took active steps against Germany.[14]

Ambrosio stuck to his guns, however. He insisted that the Tarvisio agreement must be adhered to, and he rejected the continually repeated allegations that Italian troops were in the Alps for the purpose of occupying the frontier fortifications. The German High Command felt obliged to instruct Army Group B (Rommel) to instruct lower formations that agreements must be observed and that a friendly attitude to the Italians must be maintained.[15] The allegations about Italian troop movements directed against Germany in the frontier areas that were served up to German public opinion after the Italian surrender are refuted by these official documents. The Italians never had any illusions about the ability of their weak forces in this area, which were resting after returning from operations in Russia, to offer the slightest resistance to the large number of German divisions that were pouring in.

On 11 August General Marras, the Italian Military Attaché in Berlin, informed the Germans in writing of the decision of the Comando Supremo to withdraw the Italian Fourth Army from the south of France and three divisions from the Balkans. He pointed out that it was impossible on moral and political grounds to persuade the Italian people that the great mass of Italian troops should be outside the country in this dangerous situation and that its defence should be left to German formations. Of the total of sixty-one Italian divisions, the strength and armament of which certainly did not entitle them to that designation, only twenty-four were on the Italian mainland or in Sicily, Sardinia, and

[14] Ktb. OKW, p. 912f.   [15] Ibid., p. 913.

Corsica, and of these only eleven were regular troops, and they were in need of rest and reinforcement. Another division was the militia division armed with German weapons which we have mentioned, and the other twelve were coastal defence divisions which, as the German Military Attaché had repeatedly reported, were practically useless for opposing a landing by an enemy equipped with modern weapons.[16]

This Comando Supremo communication about the intended return to Italy of Italian troops was the occasion for another meeting between the Italian military leaders and representatives of the German High Command.

General Jodl, the German Chief of Staff, accompanied by Field-Marshal Rommel, met General Roatta and General Rossi at Bologna on 15 August. Rintelen was also present. By Hitler's instructions, the external trappings of the meeting were even cruder and more hostile than they had been at Tarvisio. Providing for the security of the meeting was of course the responsibility of the host country, but strong SS formations set up a cordon round the Italian guard, and two sentries were placed directly outside the conference room. A German officer with a pistol on his belt acted as Rommel's and Jodl's personal bodyguard at lunch, and an Italian colonel, a close colleague of Rossi's, had to give up his place at table to him.

Jodl refused to drink the coffee he was offered, as Hitler had warned him against the possibility of its being poisoned. It is hard to imagine that it would have occurred to the Italians to hazard their country's future for the sake of murdering one or two German generals. Had they done so, it would have meant a quick and bloody end for the Italian government and the Italian army.

Jodl spoke very sharply to the Italians. We already knew that on returning from a tour of inspection of troops in the Caucasus he had incurred Hitler's displeasure because he had praised the local German command and troops without finding serious fault with anything.[17]

At his next mission away from headquarters he created the impression of being determined to adopt a bullying tone from the

[16] Ibid., p. 949; Badoglio, p. 69.

[17] This clash between Hitler and Jodl on 7.9.1942 and its consequences are described in Lage, pp. 11–12, and in Warlimont, pp. 267 and 268. There is also a full account in Heusinger, *Befehl im Widerstreit*, Tübingen and Stuttgart, 1950, pp. 197–200, though the incident is antedated to August 1942.

start. When the return of the Italian army from the south of France was discussed, he asked whether these troops were to be used on the Brenner. Roatta replied that he did not propose to answer tendentious questions.

An angry discussion ensued about the dissensions on the Brenner. Roatta vigorously denied all the reiterated accusations about the occupation of fortifications and the bringing up of explosive charges. No instructions for any such thing had ever been given in Rome.

Jodl, with the aid of two maps, then explained the German intentions in regard to the bringing in of more troops. He outlined the redeployment of Italian and German units in Italy that the Germans wanted, and the proposed new arrangements for quartering German troops. This made it clear that German troops were indeed to be kept massed in Upper Italy.

Roatta also produced a map showing the Comando Supremo proposals for the future deployment of German and Italian troops, and Jodl said that a comparison of the maps showed no essential differences.[18] But subsequently, after the Italian surrender, a different story was produced. According to official statements issued by the German High Command on 23 October 1943, the following remarkable statement about Roatta's map was made: 'The officers of the General Staff saw at first sight that the traitors in fact aimed at handing over the German divisions to the enemy.'[19] Goebbels also used this crude distortion of the facts in his later propaganda against Italy.[20]

Apart from Jodl's substantiated statement, General von Rintelen also testifies that there could have been no question of Roatta's map creating any such impression among the Germans at Bologna. In his memoirs he actually quotes Rommel as remarking that Roatta had made reasonable proposals for further co-operation.[21]

A man of Roatta's acumen is hardly likely to have revealed hostile intentions towards the Germans on a map. If the Italians had wanted to deploy their divisions with a view to cutting off the Germans, for which they did not have the strength, instead of disclosing their intention in this way they would have tried to make the necessary troop movements unobserved. It has also been shown that at Bologna Roatta had not yet been initiated into

---

[18] Ktb. OKW, p. 951.   [19] *Deutsche Allgemeine Zeitung*, 23.10.1943, p. 5.
[20] In *Das Reich*, 10.10.1943.   [21] Rintelen, p. 224.

other carefully considered and prepared measures planned by the King, Badoglio, and Guariglia.[22]

In accordance with Hitler's wish, stated in his instructions to Jodl, the Bologna conversations led to no improvement in German–Italian relations. Ambition alone must have made Roatta want his mission to be successful, i.e. to result in a normalization of German–Italian co-operation. He was actually being considered at the time as a possible successor to Alfieri as Italian Ambassador in Berlin. That is another reason why his objective at Bologna can have been only to diminish tension. General von Rintelen reports that on the way to Bologna Roatta and his suite were in a pretty confident mood, but were very depressed on the way back.[23]

The Bologna meeting destroyed the Italian government's and military leaders' last hope of establishing satisfactory relations with the Germans.

All over the country German divisions, far superior in strength, stood ready to act against them. Sicily was evacuated on 17 August. In preparation for the allied invasion of the mainland, air raids on all the big cities of Italy, with the exception of Rome, which the Italian government had unilaterally declared to be an open city on 15 August, began taking place on a shattering scale. The Italians were faced with the prospect of an invasion which by all military calculations was bound to be successful and must therefore lead to the destruction of all that remained of belligerent Italy.

The end of Italy as a short-term external bulwark of Germany was in sight. The only choice open to the King and Badoglio was between acceptance of the destruction of their country and the risk of approaching the allies under the cocked rifles of the Germans.

On 27 July the German Ambassador to the Holy See, Freiherr von Weizsäcker, had reported the Under-Secretary of State in the Vatican as saying: 'Badoglio's task is insoluble, for he has neither the means to continue the war nor a way of ending it.'[24]

So far from appreciating Italy's predicament, Hitler merely ignored it. His political philosophy and his fears made him kindle hostility and hate at the expense of German military interests. He rejected all the Badoglio government's efforts to secure frank discussions, and the consequence could not be in doubt.

[22] Deakin, p. 513, footnote.   [23] Rintelen, p. 245.
[24] A.A. Pol. Arch., Italien, Vol. 14, No. 72627.

The road to the armistice

The final breach between Nazi Germany and monarchist Italy took place on 8 September 1943. By a strange coincidences, this event surprised the Germans and the Italians as much as 25 July did. The Italians had been counting on a later announcement of the armistice that had been negotiated with the allies, and when it came earlier than expected they were put in considerable difficulties.

The events that led up to 8 September can be regarded as the development of the inevitable Italian response to the German attitude. Also there was an ever-growing awareness of the certainty of defeat. The documents now available make possible an exact reconstruction of the progression of events. They will be easier to follow if the story is divided into four parts: (*a*) the period of false reports and the first approaches; (*b*) the new government's plans; (*c*) the soundings; (*d*) the negotiations.

(*a*) *The period of false reports and the first approaches*

In every war in modern history the first peace feelers have been made at latest when a state of equilibrium between the two sides has existed for some time or when one side has been faced with the prospect of decisive defeat; also there have nearly always been earlier attempts at mediation, generally immediately after the outbreak of war. Immediately after the German invasion of Poland and the British declaration of war on Germany, Mussolini approached the British government in a last effort to save the peace. His efforts failed, as Hitler wanted this war, particularly as Ribbentrop, his expert on British affairs, had assured him that Britain would not fight. Also German patriots used their connections and made their good offices secretly available during the early war years in order in the interests of Germany to end what had become a war on several fronts. Some events in 1943 must be mentioned to throw light on the prehistory of the Italian surrender.

On 15 May 1943 the German Legation in Berne sent a telegram to Berlin saying it had heard from reliable sources that the Italian government was engaging in preliminary conversations with the British and the Americans with a view to extricating Italy from the war. The negotiations were being conducted by Ciano through the Vatican. The information was being checked.

On 28 May a telegram from the Legation in Berne reached Berlin saying that Italy had inquired about peace terms through an intermediary in Washington.[25] Both reports were based on false information.

There are many references in Italian memoirs to the Italian Crown Princess, who sought out contacts with known opponents of the Fascist régime and wanted Mussolini's downfall and an end of the war. She approached Bonomi and Scuero, the State Secretary at the War Ministry, but said that her husband, the Prince of Piedmont, was not prepared to take any action without his father's consent.[26]

In October 1942 she visited her brother, the King of the Belgians. The German secret service suspected her of making efforts to secure a separate peace for Italy.[27]

She also approached Badoglio, whom Mussolini had put on the retired list, and tried to persuade him to act, but he refused. He said that as a private individual without an organization he could do nothing.[28] Guariglia states that some time before 25 July 1943 she tried to make contact with Portuguese politicians with a view to opening the way to peace negotiations.[29] For a long time the King knew nothing about his daughter-in-law's efforts in this respect and, when they first came to his knowledge at the beginning of August 1943, he delivered a severe rebuke. On the 9th of that month he categorically informed her that 'in the House of Savoy women had no business in any circumstances to interfere in affairs of State'.[30]

It is surprising and of great interest to note that the only Italian peace feeler worthy of the name before 25 July was initiated by Bastianini, the head of the Italian Foreign Ministry, with Mussolini's knowledge.[31] Bastianini describes in his memoirs a conversation with the Cardinal Secretary of State Maglione on the evening of 17 July,[32] to whom he gave a very full account of the Italian situation, on the basis of which the Vatican was authorized to find out whether the allies were willing to negotiate with Italy and whether they had any ideas how negotiations could take place.

[25] Ibid., Vol. 13. Nos. 124319 and 124432   [26] Bonomi, pp. xxvii and 10.
[27] MGFA DZ, Akte W o 1–7/285.
[28] Vanna Vailati, *Badoglio racconta*, Turin, 1956, p. 359; Badoglio, p. 56.
[29] Guariglia, p. 573.   [30] Puntoni, p. 152.   [31] Deakin, p. 395; Guariglia, p. 574.
[32] Giuseppe Bastianini, *Uomini, Cose, Fatti*, Vitagliano, 1959, p. 117 f.

Bastianini actually asked the Cardinal Secretary of State for a Vatican passport for his emissary, a Rome banker named Fummi.

The passport was duly issued, and Fummi used it to travel to Lisbon, where he was to procure a British visa to go to England and see the Foreign Secretary, Mr. Eden, as he then was. He was kept waiting for his visa, however, and he was still in Lisbon when he was surprised by the events of 25 July. As Bastianini lost office with the fall of Mussolini's government, Fummi felt he had no authority to continue his mission and broke it off. Deakin states that Bastianini informed the King through the Duke of Acquarone of his conversations with Cardinal Maglione.[33]

In assessing the later actions of the Badoglio government it is important to bear in mind that the first official attempt to open the way to secret negotiations with the allies was made by the Mussolini government.

(b) The new government's plans

The King was of course very well aware that large sections of the Italian people associated Mussolini's fall with hopes of an early peace. He was also very well aware of all the obstacles that stood in the way. The first essential was to gain time. In particular, it was essential to find out how Hitler was going to react.

Of his attitude on 25 July Deakin writes: 'It was undoubtedly the express decision of the King to insist on the continuance, at any rate for the time being, of the German alliance, and even if his ultimate intention was to negotiate with the Anglo-Americans, he would need German military support in the south in order to hold the front long enough to be able to negotiate "with honour".'[34]

No doubt Badoglio's attitude when he took office was similar. In any case, the King dictated to him from the outset all the measures that he should take, as well as all his appointments to ministerial office.

Ambrosio and Acquarone had hoped to the last that the task of disengagement from the Germans would be undertaken by Mussolini,[35] and of course they expected the new government to grapple with this problem in the right way and at the right time. After 25 July, however, Ambrosio did not at first press in this direction. He was better aware than anyone else of the disproportion between

---

[33] Deakin, p. 396.   [34] Ibid., p. 499.   [35] Ibid., p. 345.

German and Italian strength. He presented Marshal Badoglio with very sober information on the subject.[36]

Wide circles in the Italian officers' corps, in particular the staff of the Comando Supremo, and the army, navy, and air force staffs as well as those of the armies in the south of France and the Balkans, genuinely believed that the Germans would acknowledge that the military weight of Italy would be increased by liberation from the corrupt Fascist régime, and some of them associated with this the hope that in these circumstances there might be a greater willingness to negotiate on the allied side. At the same time they firmly adhered to the principle of *insieme con voi* ('together with you') continually repeated to us by Montezemolo and our numerous other Italian contacts. They could conceive of the final stage of the war only in agreement with Germany.

A German Foreign Ministry memorandum on events in Italy dated 13 August 1943 also refers to the question of Italian honour. It said that 'any solution irreconcilable with Italian honour that would again make it a subject of international discussion is categorically and emphatically rejected'.[37]

The key to the attitude of many Italians in positions of civilian or military responsibility during those days of July and August was the idea that it would be possible to discuss the situation rationally with the German leadership. The words *la guerra continua* in Badoglio's proclamation represented, at any rate in regard to Italian participation in the struggle, a limited-term intention. Ways and means of bringing the war to an end must be discussed frankly with the Germans, many believed. There was a broad gamut of conjectures, most of them far too optimistic, about the conclusions the German government would draw from the changes in Italy. The greatest optimists, as conversations with Castellano, for instance, had shown, looked to Germany's following the Italian example. Some even believed that the imminent loss of Sicily would cause the Germans to give up the struggle. Guariglia quoted Clausewitz's dictum that a war must be ended when the conditions for its continuation are harder to bear than the peace terms.[38]

There was a considerable body of opinion that thought it possible that the Germans might allow Italy to withdraw into neutrality, and envisaged an agreement with them about the withdrawal of German troops from Italy. The Germans could avoid

[36] Badoglio, p. 87.   [37] Deakin, p. 519 f.   [38] Guariglia, p. 558.

suffering heavy losses in defensive operations against superior allied forces advancing step by step all the way up the Italian peninsula by withdrawing to a shorter and much stronger front in the Alps. They could then entrench themselves in their fortress and await their promised miracle weapons and the split in the allied camp prophesised by Hitler and Goebbels. Guariglia remarks in his memoirs that belief in these miracle weapons had long since died out in Italy, though in Germany it was still very much alive.[39]

Deakin also comes to the conclusion that the new Italian government did not at first exclude the possibility that the Germans might be persuaded to agree to Italy's opening peace negotiations. Hence the Badoglio government began by pursuing the policy of the Mussolini government after the Feltre conversations. It wanted to talk openly to Hitler, which Mussolini had failed to do. That was why it proposed a meeting between the King, Badoglio, and Hitler.

Rommel is known to have advocated a rapid abandonment of the Italian boot on military grounds, though he favoured a defensive position in the Apennines rather than the Alps. After 25 July the German Army General Staff carefully studied the question and also favoured a defence line in the northern Apennines.[40] But the new Italian government would never have consented to being cut off from the industrial areas of north Italy. After a short time the German leadership dropped the idea of withdrawal because of the threat of the raids on south Germany and the Rumanian oil fields which the enemy air forces would immediately have been able to carry out from bases in south Italy.

During the last months of the war Hitler himself is said to have stated that it would perhaps have been better if Italy had been completely evacuated at that time.[41]

At all events, the King and Badoglio's government were convinced that the impact of the upheaval in Italy and the outcome of the ensuing conversations with the German government must be awaited before the next steps could be decided on. Their objective was an early armistice for Italy without open conflict with the Germans.

Badoglio himself stated that he wanted to get the Germans to

[39] Ibid., p. 557.   [40] Warlimont, pp. 381, 386, and 395.
[41] Walter Hagen, *Die geheime Front*, Zürich, 1950, pp. 297 and 398.

appreciate the total impossibility of Italy's continuing the war for any length of time. This too implied the intention of arriving at an agreement with them. This statement of Badoglio's is the more significant in view of the fact that in other respects he makes great efforts in his memoirs to antedate his decision that Italy must disengage herself. In the last years of his life he tried strenuously to defend himself against charges that he did not from the outset work with sufficient determination and energy to extricate Italy quickly from the war.

The extreme view that an armistice should be sought from the allies immediately after Mussolini's fall was represented by Castellano, who since 1942 had consistently urged that Italy should extricate herself from the disastrous war as quickly as possible. As 'General for Special Employment' at the Comando Supremo he had little direct responsibility and he was therefore able to express his views more freely than others. His memoirs provide important evidence to show that the King did not associate Mussolini's dismissal with the idea of ending the war immediately. Castellano in fact complains that when the upheaval came no plans and preparations for such a step were ready.[42]

Guariglia was in a special situation. In Ankara, not knowing the position, he regarded Mussolini's fall as implying that Italy wished to conclude a separate peace immediately. In Rome a few days later he recognized the obstacles that lay in the way of a separate peace.

To sum up, then, it is clear that before 25 July or during the days that immediately followed neither the King nor Badoglio nor the members of his new government nor the military leaders made any approaches to the allies.

Statements to the contrary are attributable to false reports by German foreign missions or are inventions of Goebbels's propaganda or baseless conjectures by Hitler. Examples are telegrams from the German Legations in Lisbon and Berne of 29 July and from the Legation in Helsinki on 30 July 1943.[43]

(c) The soundings

By any normal standards the actions, gestures, and statements by the German leadership from 26 July onwards were interpretable

---

[42] Castellano, L'armistizio, p. 195 f.
[43] A.A. Pol. Arch., Italien, Vol. 14, Nos. 72600, 72630-2, and 72661; Goebbels, p. 372; Ktb. OKW, p. 854.

only as implying that Hitler was preparing to break off relations with Italy. The Italians, however, were at first willing to regard them merely as a first dismayed reaction to the inglorious end of the Fascist epoch. They were soon forced to change their minds. An entry in Puntoni's diary dated 30 July marks the point of departure of Italian approaches to the allies: 'At 5 p.m. Badoglio and Guariglia were received by the King at their urgent request. The question discussed was whether or not it was appropriate for us to make an approach to the Anglo-Americans with a view to the conclusion of a separate peace. The still threatening attitude of the Germans made the situation extremely delicate and dangerous. The King gave his approval to the Marshal's and Guariglia's proposal.'[44]

Guariglia states in his memoirs that this discussion at the Quirinal took place only on 31 July, and says that he proposed soundings with a view to concluding an armistice, not a separate peace.[45] Vanna Vailati claims that the King and Badoglio came to the conclusion that this was necessary on 28 July.[46] This is certainly wrong. Badoglio himself states that for his part he decided to sound out the allies on 29 July.[47]

Whether agreement between the King, Badoglio, and Guariglia was reached on 30 or 31 July is hard to decide. In spite of the usual accuracy of Puntoni's diary, 31 July seems the more probable date, because Guariglia produces evidence of his preparatory conversations on the previous day, 30 July. The question is relatively unimportant, however, though every day's delay underlines the patience and good faith of the Italians, who were continually receiving additional information about the stab in the back being prepared for them in the form of Operation Student.

The driving forces behind the approach to the allies were Guariglia and Castellano. The young general approached Guariglia, who had reached Rome only the evening before, on 30 July and, with Ambrosio's knowledge, gave him one of the many memoranda in which he described the hopelessness of the military situation and recommended overtures to the allies.

Guariglia agrees that, though he was still uninformed about all the details of the situation, he was convinced when he assumed

[44] Puntoni, p. 148.   [45] Guariglia, p. 585 f.
[46] Vanna Vailati, *Badoglio risponde*, Milan, 1960, p. 99.
[47] Badoglio, p. 78.

office that there was no alternative for Italy but *cambiare strada* ('to change route'). He gives his reasons as follows:

Acknowledgment of defeat after a tragedy so heroically lived through and suffered by a whole people involved neither dishonour nor coward-ice. It involved only the thorny task of saving the country from total devastation, not abandoning the hope of later reconstruction, and not giving the enemy an excuse for further irreparable destruction and revenge measures. Everyone has the right to commit suicide if he believes that his sense of honour allows him no alternative, but no one entrusted with responsibility for his country's fate has the right to drive a whole nation to suicide on the pretext that honour demands a dia-bolical persistence in an error committed by a single individual or governing class. The stronger a politician's sense of honour, the more ready must he be to sacrifice it in his country's interests, just as a hero who believes he has gained himself much glory in warfare must be ready to sacrifice that glory in order to restore peace to his country.[48]

In view of Italy's dependence on Germany, Guariglia recog-nized that the prospects of peace at first sight seemed Utopian. Nevertheless as Foreign Minister he regarded it as his duty 'to try something'. His first task was therefore to seek a conversation with 'one of the few German politicians who appreciated the extreme acuteness of the situation'.[49] Thus he began his period of office with a typical two-pronged policy, working to secure an early end of the war and at the same time to secure German appreciation of what he was doing.

On the basis of the information available in Rome about Ger-man behaviour since 25 July, he quickly decided to secure the King's and Badoglio's consent to putting out feelers towards the allies. Under the impact of the Comando Supremo's grim assess-ment of the situation, on 30 July he took advantage of the good offices of Cardinal Secretary of State Maglione to make an ap-proach to the British Minister to the Holy See, Sir D'Arcy Osborne. But the only result of this was that he discovered that this channel could not be used, because the cipher used by the British Ministry to the Vatican had been broken by the Italians and the American envoy to the Vatican had no radio transmitter.[50]

After securing the royal consent, Guariglia entrusted the Marchese Blasco Lanza D'Ajeta, the Counsellor at the Italian

[48] Guariglia, p. 558f.   [49] Ibid., p. 557 f.   [50] Ibid., p. 586.

Embassy to the Holy See, with the task of making contact with the allies in Lisbon.

D'Ajeta, who was on good terms with the Americans through his American mother, left Rome on 2 August and arrived in Lisbon next day. On 4 August at 11.30 a.m. he was received by the British Ambassador, Sir Ronald Campbell, and a first conversation took place. In accordance with his instructions, he described the desperate Italian position. He said that the powerful German forces that had been poured into Italy made it impossible for her by herself to carry out the people's wish to end the war immediately. He also mentioned that the Germans might attempt at any moment to seize the royal family and the government, which was thus forced for the time being not to change its attitude towards the Germans. To gain time and avoid rousing suspicion, a meeting between Ribbentrop and Guariglia was going to take place in a few days' time. Italy could extricate herself from the war only if the allies gave her the necessary support. The Badoglio government therefore suggested negotiations with this in view. He had no authority to negotiate, but only to propose negotiations, but he had been instructed to request at this early stage that air raids on Italy should be limited exclusively to military objectives and should be on a scale not greater than absolutely essential.

D'Ajeta's report on his conversations in Lisbon is quoted in full in Guariglia's memoirs.[51] In it he admits that he exceeded his instructions on one point. He expressed the personal opinion that Italy would declare war on Germany if she were given sufficient allied support. Also he gave very accurate information about the strength and deployment of German troops in Italy. This was very dubious behaviour at this first stage of cautious feelers, when it could not yet be known whether they would lead to further contacts.

Campbell replied that allied military plans for the further conduct of the war had been fixed for some considerable time; and, in the political respect, the formula of unconditional surrender applied to all enemy states.

Guariglia was profoundly disappointed at this outcome of his first approach. 'D'Ajeta's initiative remained a dead scrap of paper at the foot of the wall that the allies had erected with their stupid formula of unconditional surrender,' he writes.[52] The Badoglio

[51] Ibid., pp. 587–99.   [52] Ibid., p. 599.

government nevertheless hoped for signs of allied encouragement that would enable conversations to be continued.

On 5 August it sent another Foreign Ministry official, Alberto Berio, to make contact with the British Minister in Tangiers. Berio also asked that air raids on Italy should be reduced, and he also suggested that the allies should consider making landings in Europe on a broad front, in France and in the Balkans, for instance, to split up the German strength. He also asked that the allied press should continue its attacks on the Badoglio government, to avert German suspicions.

The allies made Berio wait a long time for an answer. Then, on 13 August, he was informed that Italy must first surrender, after which she would be given honourable terms. On 17 August he was informed that he must offer unconditional surrender in writing before further steps could be taken.

Guariglia also sent Alberto Pirelli to Switzerland in the first few days of August to inquire whether the Berne government would be prepared to act as an intermediary in conversations with the allies. But the head of the political department of the Swiss Foreign Ministry stated that his government was unable to do this. Switzerland was surrounded by German troops, which would immediately invade the country if such a step became known.[53]

Thus the only result of the three approaches made in the first half of August was reiteration of the allied demand for unconditional surrender. In spite of D'Ajeta's and Berio's appeals that bombings of Italian cities should cease, a very heavy raid on Milan took place on 12 August.

At this point we must revert for a moment to Guariglia's conversation with Ribbentrop at Tarvisio on 6 August, when he gave his government's word that no negotiations with the enemy were in progress. But D'Ajeta had talked to Sir Ronald Campbell in Lisbon on 4 August and Berio had arrived in Tangiers on the evening of 5 August.

If we are to engage in hair-splitting, it could be argued that these steps did not amount to negotiations, but merely to soundings But, when Ribbentrop asked whether negotiations with the enemy had begun, his questions certainly also implied soundings. In his memoirs Guariglia defends the statement he made to the Germans as follows: 'To avoid further misfortune for the country and save

[53] Ibid., p. 606 f.

K

what could still be saved there was no alternative but conceal-
ment, however hateful and repellent that may have been.'[54]

Badoglio says that he took responsibility for the approach to the
allies, and all the resulting consequences in behaviour to his
previous German ally, under the principle of *salus patriae suprema
lex*.[55]

The soundings and the negotiations that followed were kept
secret both from the Germans and from the Italian people until
the surprise announcement of the armistice on 8 September 1943
because only very few individuals were initiated and because the
King, Badoglio, and Guariglia determinedly kept their German
partner in the dark. Because of what was at stake they did not
shrink from giving their word of honour when they were asked
very precise and specific questions.

(d) The negotiations

The fourth approach was made on 12 August. The German
leaders had still made no conciliatory move towards the Badoglio
government. The conversations at Tarvisio had finally persuaded
the Italians that the Germans were either unwilling or unable to
save Italy from the abyss, and they believed them to be systematically continuing preparations to seize power in Italy.

As reference had been made in D'Ajeta's soundings in Lisbon
to a possible distinction between political and military agreements,
this time Rome decided to send a soldier.[56] The choice fell on
Castellano. The latter says that the instructions given him by
Guariglia and Ambrosio were vague. As a precautionary measure
he was given no powers. All he had was a brief letter of introduction from the British Minister to the Holy See, and his task was
made more difficult by the fact that he was told nothing about the
preceding approaches made by D'Ajeta, Berio, and Pirelli.[57] That
is a further illustration of the extreme degree of discretion with
which Badoglio, Guariglia, and Ambrosio set about their task.
The King had imposed the greatest secrecy; even the Prince of
Piedmont was not initiated, and Puntoni, the King's aide-de-
camp, knew nothing of what was going on. The entry in his diary
on 8 September, the day of the armistice, was: 'Only just now, at
5 p.m., did I find out, and only in the most general way, that

[54] Ibid., p. 609.
[55] Badoglio, p. 78. ('The country's welfare is the supreme law.')
[56] Guariglia, p. 640.   [57] Castellano, *L'armistizio*, p. 87 f.

contacts with the Anglo-Americans were taken up several days ago.'[58]

Castellano reached Madrid by a devious route at midday on 15 August. He crossed the frontiers in the guise of a foreign exchange official. He succeeded in seeing the British Ambassador, Sir Samuel Hoare, on the same afternoon, and with greater frankness and purposefulness than his predecessors he declared Italy's willingness to stop fighting the allies and turn her weapons against the Germans. Guariglia had not given him such far-reaching instructions, and he later blamed himself for thus taking things into his own hands. But he seems to have had Ambrosio's agreement to what he said.[59]

Badoglio and Guariglia sought throughout to conduct the negotiations in such a way as to avoid immediate hostilities with the Germans.[60]

The gist of Castellano's further conversations with Sir Samuel Hoare and the conversation with Sir Ronald Campbell, the British Ambassador in Lisbon, that followed, was his attempt to persuade the allies to reveal their strategic intentions in regard to the Italian mainland, so that the Italians could adjust themselves to them. Castellano said that he had no authority to make proposals for allied operations.

There are contradictory statements about whether Castellano did or did not discuss the strength and deployment of German troops in Italy with Sir Samuel Hoare and Sir Ronald Campbell. Castellano says that he did not do so; as a soldier it was his duty to observe military secrecy while soundings were in these early stages.[61] Hoare states, however, that Castellano was 'willing' to give information of this nature and mentioned the presence of fifteen German divisions on Italian soil.[62]

The allies gathered from the Italian approach that they were willing to surrender only if they were given sufficient support against the Germans. The Italians expressed the hope that about fifteen Anglo-American divisions would invade the peninsula simultaneously with a cease-fire. They sought information about the allied plans in order to ensure protection for their government

[58] Puntoni, p. 161.   [59] Castellano, *L'armistizio*, pp. 84 and 86, and 125.
[60] Kurt von Tippelskirch, *Geschichte des Zweiten Weltkriegs*, Frankfurt and Bad Godesberg, 1951, p. 367; Castellano, p. 126.
[61] Castellano, *L'armistizio*, p. 93.
[62] Sir Samuel Hoare, *Ambassador on Special Mission*, London, 1946, p. 213.

and their cities, but they were refused this information on security grounds.[63]

Castellano too had his patience severely tried in Lisbon. Not till 19 August did the next conversation take place at the British Ambassador's residence. Also present were General Eisenhower's Chief of Staff, General Bedell Smith, General Strong, and Mr. George Kennan as political adviser. General Bedell Smith, without beating about the bush, presented what in the circumstances were General Eisenhower's twelve extremely hard terms on which the Italians could have an armistice. The essential points were: cessation of hostilities against the allies; cessation of support for the Germans; the handing over of all British and American prisoners; the handing over of the Italian fleet and air force to the allies so that they might be disarmed; the handing over of the merchant fleet; provision of bases for allied military operations on the mainland and the islands; local protection of these bases to be provided by Italian forces; the ordering home of Italian forces stationed outside Italy; the use of force for the maintenance of these conditions should the necessity arise; acceptance of allied administrative measures on Italian territory; recognition of the allied right to take measures for disarmament, demobilization, and demilitarization. Conditions of a political, economic, and financial nature were to be submitted later.

Castellano believed he had initiated negotiations for an Italian transfer from the German to the allied side, but not that he had asked for an armistice, and he was therefore surprised when he was presented with armistice terms. He said he must report back to Rome. At the same time he pointed out that some of the conditions were unfulfillable, because Italy was dominated by German troops.

Castellano was also informed by Bedell Smith of the contents of a supplementary telegram from Roosevelt and Churchill in Quebec. According to this, these armistice terms would be modified according to the amount of support received by the allies from the Italian government and people during the remainder of the war.[64]

General Bedell Smith's communication of these terms to Castellano and the latter's submission of them to his government completed the transition from the phase of soundings to that of negotiations.

[63] Dwight D. Eisenhower, *Crusade in Europe*, London, 1949, p. 203.
[64] Castellano, *L'armistizio*, p. 110; Guariglia, p. 663.

Castellano arrived back in Rome on the morning of 27 August,[65] though it has often been stated in the literature on the subject that he reached there only on 28 August.[66] To their immense disappointment, Badoglio, Guariglia, and Ambrosio could see in the terms he brought back nothing better for Italy than unconditional surrender. Thus at the time of Castellano's return a nadir was reached in the situation of the Italian government, and it had to use its last efforts in an attempt to escape from it. On the German side the way was blocked, as before. There was no way out in that direction for the Italians, except the prospect of being used up as cannon-fodder.

So during the last days of August the King and his closest associates had no alternative but to reconcile themselves to agreeing to continue negotiations on the basis of the allied terms.

On 31 August Castellano flew to Sicily for a few hours to see General Bedell Smith. He was to seek alleviation of the allied terms and, above all, assurances of a large-scale allied operation against the Italian mainland at the time of the announcement of the armistice. The allies remained tough. They declined the Italian request that their fleet might be sent to Sardinia, i.e. not to allied ports. Bedell Smith repeatedly threatened to break off negotiations in the event of further haggling.

On the afternoon of 1 September the King accepted Badoglio's advice that the armistice must be signed. On 2 September Castellano again flew to Sicily, this time accompanied by Major Marchesi, and the armistice was signed on the afternoon of 3 September.

In the final phase of the negotiation the allies went some way to meeting the Italians on one point only. They agreed to drop parachute troops and land an armoured task force near Rome at the time of the announcement of the armistice, but this was never done. An allied senior officer who was sent secretly to Rome on a reconnaissance mission found the situation there so confused that it seemed impossible to assure the co-operation with Italian troops that would be essential.

The allied announcement of the armistice on 8 September took the Italians by surprise. This may have been due to some last-minute misunderstanding in the negotiations that had to be conducted so cautiously. In these circumstances the King, Badoglio

[65] Castellano, L'armistizio, p. 125; Guariglia, p. 663.
[66] Deakin, p. 528; Badoglio, p. 92.

and their advisers anxiously debated on the evening of 8 September whether or not to acknowledge and announce it. In the last vital debate presided over by the King, the young Major Marchesi passionately argued against further delay and insisted that the path on which they had struck out must be continued even in these more difficult circumstances.

The Germans succeeded in gaining possession of Rome within twenty-four hours. The five weak Italian divisions deployed in very improvised defensive positions round the capital surrendered on 9 September, when Field-Marshal Kesselring, at the suggestion of Major-General Westphal, his Chief of Staff, offered them very honourable conditions for the laying down of their arms. Thus Rome was spared, and a parting of former allies took place without bloodshed.

The King and the government left Rome on the night of 8–9 September. Puntoni describes how hard it was for the King to take this step. But he wanted to preserve his freedom of action, so that he could continue the contact now made with the allies for his country's benefit. Also he wanted to save Rome from the horrors of war that would no doubt have descended on it if the government had remained.[67]

The King's behaviour is still criticized in Italy and also in the former allied countries. It is often argued that he should have stayed in Rome and allowed himself to become a martyr in German hands, and that fleeing from Rome damaged the reputation of the House of Savoy and the monarchical idea in Italy. But, if one looks at the demands of the hour, it was certainly in the interests of all Italians and all Italian territory outside the German grip that after 8 September the King should represent their interests in relation to the allies. He could do this with more weight than the improvised Badoglio government would have had alone.

With the transfer of the Italian government to the south the process of extricating Italy from the war with the allies was formally concluded.

The broken treaty

The smoking ruins in Germany in the spring of 1945 provided the King, Badoglio, and their colleagues with confirmation that in

[67] Puntoni, p. 164 f.

1943 they acted in their country's interests. Many who had previously accused them of treachery to an ally, of treaty-breaking, and of shameful capitulation now had second thoughts.

There is no question of treachery on their part, but only too much evidence of the German leadership's breach of faith to its so much weaker ally before the latter turned to the Anglo-Americans.

On 7 November 1943 General Jodl, speaking to German national leaders and Gauleiters in Munich, said of the events in Italy: 'We had to avoid doing anything to give the Italians a moral excuse for their treachery or by premature hostile action actually to commit treachery ourselves.'[68] These words in themselves provide justification for Badoglio's action. A government threatened with an assault of the nature of Operation Student cannot be denied the moral right to draw the conclusions that seem appropriate to it. It is certainly under no obligation to feel any bond of loyalty to an ally that makes plans and preparations to throttle it. Plans and preparations in such an instance are morally equivalent to the act itself. It would have been an unpardonable and irresponsible neglect of duty to remain inactive in the face of such a threat to a government approved by the people and to the whole country.

The basis of the German–Italian brotherhood in arms was provided by the pact of friendship and alliance between Germany and Italy, generally known as the Pact of Steel, of 22 May 1939. The vital stipulation that forbade the making of a separate peace was Article V: 'The contracting parties undertake in the event of conducting war together to conclude an armistice or peace only in complete agreement with each other.'[69]

It has been claimed that Mussolini's downfall and the collapse of Fascism invalidated the Pact of Steel and thus relieved Italy of her obligations. Bonomi says in this connection: 'Fortunately the treaty of alliance had an unusual preamble. It said that this was not an alliance between two states and peoples, but between two régimes, two revolutions. Thus the collapse of the Fascist régime made the alliance void.'[70]

Even though this conclusion was drawn by such an experienced statesman as Bonomi, who was twice Prime Minister, the argument

[68] Gert Buchheit, *Hitler der Feldherr*, Rastatt, 1958, p. 355.
[69] ADAP, D, Vol. VI, p. 466, Document No. 426.
[70] Bonomi, p. 6.

is rather dubious. The parties to the treaty identified their régime with the state and the people. They intended to contract an alliance between the two nations, and made use of their revolutionary terminology in expressing this intention. Thus Bonomi's interpretation does not take into account the meaning that the parties to the alliance themselves attributed to it, and is not reconcilable with the elementary principle of international law *pacta sunt servanda* ('treaties must be kept').

Instead one must proceed on the assumption that, according to international law and all precedents, the Badoglio government as the legal successor to Mussolini's government assumed all the international obligations undertaken by the latter. There are, however, two other considerations that raise the question whether the Badoglio government was bound by the Pact of Steel. In 1939 it was an open secret that the Reich government pressed Italy, which was far from being ready for war, to sign the pact, and to reassure it undertook not to create any warlike situations for several years. Knowledge of this undertaking was so widespread that it was often assumed that it was contained in a secret appendix to the treaty. Thus Grandi writes: 'I knew that the Pact of Steel contained a secret clause in which Hitler undertook not to do anything that might break the peace in the next three years.'[71] The treaty in fact contained no such secret clause. There was merely a short secret additional protocol referring to agreements that were to be withheld from publication about the setting-up of special committees and other measures in the field of press, information, and propaganda services.[72]

Examination of the assurances given by the Reich government shows the following. In the first place, Mussolini announced at a meeting of the Grand Council on 5 February 1939 that Italy could not risk war before 1942, since she must first consolidate her position in Libya, Albania, and Abyssinia. Also the building of six warships must be awaited, the army's artillery must be modernized, millions of Italians must be repatriated, Japan must master the situation in China, and the world exhibition that it was proposed to hold in Rome in 1942 must be awaited in order to raise urgently needed foreign exchange.

At a meeting in Milan on 6 May 1939 Ciano discussed this in detail with Ribbentrop. The German Foreign Minister's reply was

---

[71] Grandi, p. 25.   [72] ADAP, D, Vol. 6, p. 468 f.

that Germany too needed four or five years of peace, though if necessary she could be ready for war much sooner.

When Ciano signed the Pact of Steel in Berlin on 21 May 1939, Ribbentrop again assured him that Germany needed a long period of peace. On this occasion he spoke of 'at least three years'.[73]

At the stormy meeting of the Fascist Grand Council on 24 July 1943, Ciano made Hitler's behaviour in connection with these assurances the point of departure for a vigorous attack on Germany. Mussolini had previously spoken emotionally of Italy's being bound by her treaty obligations, but Ciano reminded him that he had signed the treaty only after Hitler had given the assurances we have described. It had turned out subsequently, however, that the German attack on Poland had been decided on, and a date for it actually fixed, before the signature of the pact. Hitler had in fact given written orders for the annexation of Danzig and for 'Operation White', i.e. the attack on Poland, many weeks previously, that is to say, on 3 April 1939.[74] Ciano pointed out that Hitler had failed to consult the Italian government in August 1939 before beginning hostilities against Poland, though under Article I and Article II, paragraph 1, of the Pact of Steel he was under an obligation to do so.

Ciano ended his indictment of Germany by declaring that a charge of betrayal could be directed only against the Germans. 'At all events, we would not be the betrayers but the betrayed.'[75]

The Italians were undoubtedly grossly deceived by Hitler's behaviour in the matter. The question arose whether the reiterated assurances they were given, though these were only verbal, were so closely associated with the treaty that the breach of undertaking could be regarded as relieving the Italians of their obligations under it. A dispatch by Ambassador von Mackensen dated 23 August 1939 is evidence that the Italian government took this view; it had informed him that in its view the Pact of Steel was based on an agreement that there would be no war until 1942 and that a German attack on Poland would constitute a breach of the treaty.[76]

To go more deeply into this question would be mere legal

[73] Wiskemann, p. 141; Galeazzo Ciano, *Diario*, p. 102, entry of 21.5.1939.

[74] Walter Hubatsch, *Hitlers Weisungen für die Kriegsführung 1939–1945, Dokumente des Oberkommandos der Wehrmacht*, Frankfurt, 1962, p. 17 f; Wiskemann, p. 143.

[75] Giuseppe Bottai, *Vent'anni e un giorno*, Milan, 1949, pp. 303 and 309 f.

[76] Kirkpatrick, p. 400.

quibbling, because the Italians did not make any practical use of the situation. By intervening in the war on Germany's side in June 1940 they showed conclusively that they did not insist on the fulfilment of this German obligation.

The so-called principle of frustration plays an important part in the domestic law of contract. It lays down that a contract ceases to be enforceable if the underlying assumptions on which it was based have lapsed or have greatly changed in a way that could not have been foreseen at the time when it was made. By universal consent the same principle applies in international law, in which the *clausula rebus sic stantibus* corresponds to the principle of frustration in domestic law. But, just as in the latter, strict standards are applied to assure adherence to the overriding principle that treaties must be adhered to.

Thus in considering German–Italian relations in the summer of 1943 the question arises whether German behaviour had not brought about such fundamental and unforeseeable changes from the point of view of Italian interests as to cause Italian obligations under the treaty to lapse. The answer, in my opinion, is that it had certainly done so. The mere disappearance of the prospects of winning the war that the two parties were fighting together would not of course suffice for an appeal to the principle of *rebus sic stantibus*. But when one party to an alliance treats the other in the way that we have described, refuses it equality of rights, tries to force it to hazard its own future by acting in a hopeless situation as a forward defence post in order to enable it to prolong its own resistance, and finally threatens to overthrow its government by the force of arms, the assumptions on which the treaty was based must be regarded as having been destroyed. Thus by international standards the Badoglio government must certainly be absolved of the charge of treaty breaking.

It has, however, been alleged that the Italian government committed a breach of the treaty by acting without informing its ally.[77]

German–Italian co-operation in the war years was characterized by the fact that German behaviour at top level excluded serious discussion of threatening dangers, including those likely to have a decisive effect on the outcome of the war. It was strictly forbidden, just as it was inside Germany, to consider the possibility of a

[77] Goebbels, p. 839.

defeat. At all German–Italian meetings only one kind of language was used, and that was the language of the German leadership, based on the certitude of final victory.

Thus at Tarvisio on 6 August 1943 Ribbentrop refused all objective discussion of dangers that 'might threaten final victory'. The German leaders were very well aware that the Italians had felt themselves to be at the end of their tether for some considerable time. They were given a perfectly clear picture of the situation by the military liaison staffs that were in contact with Italian authorities and Italian troops, by the reports of German consulates, and above all by the continuous reports of the attachés of the three services in Rome. Thus it was totally irresponsible of the German leaders to take such inadequate account of the justifiable worries of their weaker ally, whom they merely called on to have faith in victory.

Friendly relations with their ally having thus long since given way to tension, it would have been impossible and actually suicidal for the Italian government to announce that it proposed to extricate itself from the war after it had been refused even the opportunity of frankly discussing its plight. It must be borne in mind that after 25 July every move the Italians made was carried out at the point of German bayonets the use of which they dared not provoke. By the end of July and the beginning of August, or at latest at the meeting at Tarvisio, they knew for certain that any announcement of peace talks would certainly provoke those bayonets. This situation created a state of emergency. Government and people were in danger.

In domestic law inevitable necessity exonerates an individual of violation of the law if danger to life or property cannot otherwise be avoided. In international law there is a corresponding principle of self-help that applies to this or similar circumstances. Various types of this can be distinguished, e.g. self-defence, inevitable necessity, and self-protection.[78] As self-defence implies an illegal assault, the Italian action in trying to disengage themselves from the German grip by going over to the allies cannot be regarded as self-defence in the real sense of the term. According to the principle laid down by Jeschek, the Italian government was entitled to rely on the principle of inevitable necessity. Jeschek states: 'Inevitable necessity implies that a present or imminent grave danger exists

[78] Georg Dahm, *Völkerrecht* II, Stuttgart, 1961, p. 409.

that threatens the life of a state, the continued existence of its territory or its citizens or its independence, and that the danger cannot be averted except by measures contrary to international law.'[79] The measure contrary to international law here exonerated of illegality by the existence of a state of emergency is Italian violation of the Pact of Steel.

Verdross, the well-known Austrian teacher of international law, however, sees inevitable necessity as arising only if a state is forced to invade the territory of an innocent state for the purpose of defending its existence against a threatening danger. Such a state of affairs did not exist so far as Italy was concerned. Verdross takes the view, however, that a state must be granted the right to self-protection in all circumstances in which it has to defend itself against a threatening, objectively wrongful state of affairs, without invading the territory of an innocent state.[80] Georg Dahm, however, regards this as a 'not undangerous extension of the principle of self-help' which has still to be established in international practice.[81] It seems probable that a thorough examination of the international legal aspects of the way in which the Badoglio government disengaged itself from the German alliance would establish a precedent in international law for Verdross's principle of self-protection.

Whether we follow Jeschek and say that a state of inevitable necessity existed for Italy in the summer of 1943 or, like Verdross, grant her the right of self-protection, the Italian government could rely on the principle of self-help in one form or the other. That is an even stronger defence than an appeal to the principle of *rebus sic stantibus*.

So much in broad outline for the legal aspects of the situation, in so far as there is any interest in applying the yardstick of international law to the events of that time.

During the war, and also in post-war literature, the Italians were bitterly denounced for the way in which they conducted the surrender negotiations. We shall deal here with two especially grave charges that were levelled at them.

The first was that in their secret soundings and negotiations they

---

[79] Hans-Heinrich Jeschek, *Die Verantwortlichkeit der Staatsorgane nach Völkerstrafrecht*, Bonn, 1952, p. 220.
[80] Alfred Verdross, *Völkerrecht*, 4th edn, Vienna, 1959, p. 348 f.
[81] Georg Dahm, op. cit., p. 409, footnote.

offered the allies the German divisions in Italy 'as a dowry'. This charge was made in an official statement by the German High Command on the events in Italy,[82] and it is repeated by Warlimont[83] and Kesselring.[84] Inspection of the Italian and allied documents shows that it is without foundation. It is also irreconcilable with the German–Italian relations of strength at the time.

In the first place, one is entitled to ask what is meant by the suggestion that the German divisions were 'offered as a dowry'. To provide such a dowry, the Italians would have had either to attack these German divisions or to hold them until they could be handed over to the allies when the armistice came into force, or at least to cordon them off until allied troops arrived by sea or air to overpower and capture them. It would have been impossible for the Italian command to ask its troops to do any such thing. Any attempt to use them offensively against the Germans was condemned to disaster; they were war-weary and hopelessly inferior in weapons. German troops, with the help of the Luftwaffe, would have smashed all attempts to cordon them off within hours, or at most a few days. Offering the German divisions as a 'dowry' in this instance would have been equivalent to asking a watch-dog to overpower a fully grown tiger, or at least to 'hold' it until the hunter arrived.

It must also be borne in mind that the Italian troops would have set about carrying out a surprising order of this kind only very reluctantly and half-heartedly, because to a large extent they were still well-disposed to their German allies, or at any rate had a high respect for their fighting ability and modern weapons; and the Italian command was very familiar with the systematic tactics of the allies, who avoided swift and daring moves. It was very well able to calculate how long it would take them to be in a position to support and relieve the Italian troops committed against the Germans.

Mention was made during the negotiations of Italian troops taking over a security role in regard to certain installations as soon as the invasion of the mainland began. There is a vast difference between that and their engaging or handing over German troops. Castellano states that it emerged from the instructions given to him for the negotiations in Lisbon that the Italian command hoped that

[82] *Deutsche Allgemeine Zeitung*, 23.10.1943, p. 5.
[83] Warlimont, p. 388.   [84] Kesselring, p. 235.

the Germans would withdraw from central Italy to defend the Alpine passes if their lines of communication were threatened by an allied invasion.[85]

A certain exception is provided by the agreement reached shortly before the signature of the armistice on 3 September concerning joint action in regard to Rome. The Germans were not in occupation of the Italian capital, and the Italians wanted to defend it against the inevitable German attempt to seize it. They therefore asked for allied aid on the day when the armistice was announced. These were local arrangements for the defence of the capital, which was also the seat of government. But the allies failed to provide the promised aid, and the Italian divisions in the neighbourhood of Rome surrendered.

Finally, the ill-considered allegation is refuted by the behaviour of the Italian government and troops when the armistice was announced. The government ordered its armed forces to cease all hostilities against the Anglo-Americans, but 'to react against possible attacks from any other source'.[86] They were thus to behave passively, and to defend themselves only if attacked by the Germans. On 8 September and the days that followed German troops, in accordance with previously prepared plans, everywhere took action against the Italians, who in most cases were disarmed without bloodshed. In cases in which Italian units put up resistance in accordance with their government's orders, as occurred in several places in the Balkans, for instance, they were quickly overpowered. By Hitler's orders the officers of these units were disgracefully shot.

One of the victims of this arbitrary and crude violation of international law was General Antonio Gandin. He had held an important post at the Comando Supremo for many years and had taken part in the meeting at Klessheim in April. He rightly had the reputation of being well disposed towards the Germans, and spoke German fluently. On 8 September 1943 he was in command of the Acqui Division on the island of Cephalonia off the west coast of Greece. It is significant that when the armistice was announced his first decision was that hostilities with the Germans must be avoided; he considered it wrong to risk the lives of the 12,000 men under his command in the existing situation. But a number of his

[85] Castellano, *L'armistizio*, p. 92.
[86] Badoglio, p. 98.

officers, particularly the younger ones, insisted that the orders from Rome that Italian troops must defend themselves against 'attacks from other sources' must be obeyed.[87] Gandin, an intelligent but not very energetic general, was not able to resist these officers' pressure, and could not prevent a battle from taking place. The incident throws light on the hostility to Germany that had developed among the junior members of the Italian officers' corps, though the German leadership often maintained that it was only the Italian generals who stood in the way of the war against the allies and the partnership with Germany.

The other sensitive charge that has been made against the Badoglio government in connection with the surrender concerns the alleged offer to hand over Mussolini to the allies. In this connection we again quote the official statement of the German High Command of 23 October 1943. It says that 'the handing over of the Duce was agreed and planned' under the terms of the armistice of 3 September 1943.[88] Anfuso also states in his memoirs that Badoglio promised the allies to hand over Mussolini[89] In the summer of 1943 Filippo Anfuso was Italian Ambassador in Budapest, and he put himself at Mussolini's disposal again when the Italian Fascist Republic was set up in Upper Italy. He served as his ambassador in Berlin, and during the last months of the war he was State Secretary in his Foreign Ministry.

Mussolini himself stated that his handing over to the allies was agreed on in the negotiations in Lisbon in the last ten days of August.[90] He relied for this statement on Churchill's speech in the House of Commons on 21 September 1943. Churchill, in fact, made some remarks that superficially seemed to provide support for the allegations of the German High Command, Anfuso and Mussolini, because he said: 'Unconditional surrender, of course, comprises everything, but not only was a special provision for the surrender of war criminals included in the longer terms, but a particular stipulation was made for the surrender of Signor Mussolini. It was not however possible to arrange for him to be delivered specially and separately before the armistice and our main landing took place, for this would certainly have disclosed the intentions of the Italian government to the enemy who were intermingled

[87] Attilio Tamaro, *Due anni di storia, 1943–1945*, Vol. II, Rome, 1951, p. 423 f.
[88] *Deutsche Allgemeine Zeitung*, 23.10.1943, p. 5.   [89] Anfuso, p. 238.
[90] Benito Mussolini, *Geschichte eines Jahres*, 1st edn, 1945, p. 121.

with him at every point and who had them so largely in their power.'[91]

The memoirs, reports, and memoranda written by Castellano, D'Ajeta, and Berio, however, contain nothing to indicate that Mussolini's fate was mentioned during the negotiations that led to the armistice.

Moreover, the allegations about an offered or intended handing over of the Duce are hard to reconcile with the behaviour of the Italian government. On 8 August it had moved Mussolini to the island of La Maddalena, off the northern tip of Sardinia, and on 28 August he was flown from there to the Gran Sasso d'Italia, a mountain range in the Apennines north-east of Rome. The reason for moving him was generally assumed to be that the Germans had discovered the hiding-place at La Maddalena; a few days before a German aircraft had made a low-level flight over the house in which Mussolini was quartered. If the Italian government had intended or offered to hand him over to the allies, it is hardly likely that at a time when the armistice negotiations had reached such an advanced stage it would have had him removed from a hiding-place in Sardinia, which was near the allied bases, to a place in the northern half of the Italian peninsula. It would have been perfectly feasible and much more sensible to transfer him to somewhere in Sardinia or south Italy.

It was also very evident that no preparations were made to remove him from the Gran Sasso to south Italy after the announcement of the armistice or to take any other steps to facilitate his hand-over. Thus Anfuso makes a false assumption in claiming that Badoglio in the hurried flight from Rome on 8 September himself took steps to take this so valuable 'hostage' with him.[92] Also there is no scrap of evidence that the British or Americans ever reproved the Italians for having either deliberately or negligently failed to fulfil their offer or agreement to hand over Mussolini. Any such agreement, if it were made, must have been arrived at before 12 September, because afterwards it would have been pointless, for on that day the Skorzeny *coup* was carried out and Mussolini was taken from the Gran Sasso to Germany.

In the absence of other evidence or confirmation, a careful

[91] Winston Churchill, speech in House of Commons, 21.9.1943, *The Times*, London, 22.9.43.
[92] Anfuso, p. 238.

reading of Churchill's statement rouses the suspicion that he was adroitly trying to anticipate any possible awkward questions in the House. He said nothing about any Italian offer to hand over Mussolini; all he said was that a special clause referring to his handing over had been agreed on. He gave no date for it. The verbatim report of his speech on 21 September shows that he was trying to show the House that, in spite of the precipitous events that had been taking place in the Mediterranean area in the past few weeks, the government had thought of everything and had not been too soft in relation to the Italians.

So one might be misled into supposing that a riddle lay behind these contradictions. The matter is not dealt with by Deakin in his extensive survey. But a reconstruction of the three stages of the armistice negotiations clarifies the matter. On 3 September only the three briefly formulated basic allied terms were signed by General Castellano in Sicily, and Mussolini had not been mentioned in the preceding negotiations and was not mentioned in this document. But there was a clause in it that said that further stipulations connected with the armistice would be communicated to the Italians later, and that they would have to sign these. The Italian emissaries tried to object to this clause, on the ground that it implied blind acceptance of unstated conditions, but their objections were not heeded. The allies stubbornly insisted on an immediate signature, otherwise the negotiations would be broken off and the Italians would have to return to their unhappy position of being ground between two millstones. On receiving further instructions from Rome Castellano then signed the document at 5.15 p.m. on 3 September.

The additional terms were presented to him next day, 4 September, and they indeed included a demand that the Italian government should hand over Mussolini. Badoglio signed these terms during the third stage, that is, at the definitive conclusion of the armistice agreement in Malta on 29 September 1943, or seventeen days after Mussolini's abduction to Germany. General Castellano confirmed in a letter to me of 12 May 1966 that this was in fact the course of events. He emphasized that thus no offer by the Badoglio government to hand over Mussolini was ever made.

Thus Churchill was not bending the truth when he mentioned a special clause concerning the handing over of Mussolini. On 21

L

September he merely failed to mention that this clause was made known to the Italians only after the signature of the terms on 3 September and that on 21 September these had not yet been signed. All that existed was the Italian 'preliminary obligation' of 3 September to accept all the terms to be submitted to them later.

Thus Badoglio would have found it very difficult to oppose this stipulation about Mussolini when the armistice agreement was finally concluded on 29 September. However, by then the question had become academic, as Mussolini was well beyond the Italian government's reach.

We shall refer only briefly here to the unhappy role imposed on Mussolini when Hitler made him head of the puppet government in Upper Italy for the remaining nineteen months of the war. It was not only in his letter to Badoglio written on the evening of 25 July 1943 that he announced his withdrawal from the political scene. There are many indications that while he was under arrest from 25 July to 12 September he totally rejected the idea of ever engaging in politics again. When it was suggested to him that the Germans might make an attempt to free him, he flared up and said: 'That would be the greatest humiliation that could be inflicted on me. Do you really think I should want to go to Germany and try to seize the reins again with German aid? Oh no!'[93]

For all his shadowy existence at the head of the artificial Fascist rump republic in Upper Italy, it must be admitted that he unintentionally and without taking any active steps in the matter performed a service. He became the protector of the country under his control and its inhabitants. Though the notorious neo-Fascist armed gangs, the so-called *brigate nere*, committed many crimes against their fellow-countrymen, who were weary of war and political fanaticism, the presence of Mussolini prevented worse from happening. Anfuso writes: 'Mussolini was the sole bulwark against the application of the criminal SS culture. After the autumn of 1943 he diverted Hitler's attention and thus turned a people destined to be sacrificed into an ally of Germany. When the Germans wanted to pounce vengefully on the peninsula he to a large extent saved it from SS reprisals.'[94] Elsewhere he says: 'Mussolini stopped the terrestrial arm of Hitler's *vendetta* (vengeance) and put Nazi Germany in a different situation in relation to the Italians.'[95]

[93] Kirkpatrick, p. 543.   [94] Anfuso, p. 185.   [95] Ibid., p. 242.

One is forced to accept this view of Anfuso's when one reads the following entry in Goebbels's diaries dated 13 September 1943: 'So long as the Duce was not there, we had the possibility of making a *tabula rasa* in Italy. We could ruthlessly solve the problems that existed in relation to Italy. I had been thinking that, quite apart from the South Tyrol, our frontier might well be advanced to Venice. That will hardly be possible if the Duce again assumes political office. Under the Duce's leadership Italy will again try to resume a nationalist rump life towards which we are in many respects under an obligation.'[96]

On the other hand, Mussolini's reappearance sharpened the conflicts between the two separated halves of Italy. Though on the evening of 25 July he had announced his devotion and loyalty to the King, when he became Hitler's tool in the north he blamed and besmirched the King and went on doing so to the end. By this he put himself as much in the wrong as he did by tolerating the political trials of his former colleagues at Verona and Parma. Of the King, General von Senger rightly observes: 'In the Second World War Victor Emmanuel III did his people as great a service by liquidating it at the right time as he did by his determination to resist after Caporetto during the First World War. The fact that he could not take that step openly in agreement with his Nazi allies was the result of the latter's relationship to powers of quite a different kind.'[97]

Let us conclude with a very remarkable quotation from the war diary of the German High Command. In the so-called descriptive section that was added to the daily entries on the occasion of the publication of Vol. III in 1963 the following passage occurs on page 1,530: 'Also false was the description of the Italian surrender as an "act of treachery". It had long been known on the German side that Italy was at the end of her tether. In a situation that grew more and more hopeless Italy remained loyal to the Axis alliance for a full year after the failure of the last offensive in Africa. A realistic examination of the situation might have led to the realization in Germany that it would have been better to end the war jointly, with Mussolini or with Badoglio. But there was little encouragement for this from her partner; the will to destroy destroyed the possibility of an understanding.'

[96] Goebbels, p. 413 f.
[97] Frido von Senger und Etterlin, *Krieg in Europa*, Cologne, 1960, p. 190.

This retrospective assessment, particularly the first sentence, sensibly withdraws many criticism and suspicions that crept prematurely and under the influence of emotion into the daily entries in the war diary of the German High Command. The emphatic withdrawal of the nasty word 'treachery' sounds conciliatory, but a long road had to be travelled from the false statements, based on the assumption of treachery, made by the German High Command in October 1943 to the admission in this retrospective survey that such allegations were untenable.

Conclusion

On 31 August 1943 Bismarck and Rintelen were relieved of their posts.

'Among concomitant phenomena in the personal field during those days, it seems worth mentioning that the meritorious General von Rintelen was dismissed from his post on 31 August in a manner that soon became usual. His successor appeared unannounced at his door with a letter from Keitel in his hand.'[98]

Rintelen's departure from Rome was delayed. But, thanks to a pass issued by the Comando Supremo and the magnanimous help of the Italian authorities, he was actually able to leave Rome by air on 9 September, the turbulent day that followed the announcement of the armistice. This was in striking contrast to the treatment handed out to the attachés of the three Italian services in Berlin. On Hitler's instructions, and in flagrant violation of their diplomatic immunity, they were removed at Grafing, near Munich, from the train that was supposed to be taking them to the Brenner to be exchanged for their German colleagues and put under arrest. General Marras and his colleagues were taken to the headquarters of the Security Police in Berlin and kept under arrest in humiliating conditions for a long time.[99]

Here we shall merely note that, after Hitler's attack on their country in June 1941, the Russians facilitated in the most courteous manner the return to Germany by way of Turkey of the whole of the personnel of the German Embassy in Moscow, including the Military Attaché and his staff.

Bismarck and Rintelen were not employed again. General von Rintelen was actually released from the army, though the personnel office was having the greatest difficulty at the time in filling vacant generals' posts. A year later, when methods had grown

[98] Warlimont, p. 389.   [99] MGFA DZ, Akte H 27/56 and H 27/58.

even harsher, the defamation and suspicions to which they were exposed would have led to far more drastic steps being taken against them.

During the war most of the German senior military commanders asked themselves whether they were right to remain at their posts under the existing leadership. I know that General von Rintelen often pondered that question. But since 1943 he had been on terms of close trust with clear-sighted and well-intentioned Italians, and during the war years they gave many signs of the value they attached to continued co-operation with him. They hoped for his understanding and also his mediation when the expected crisis came. When one considers his contribution to the prevention of Operation Student, these hopes were fulfilled. He remained at his post in spite of internal revolt because it provided him with opportunities of diminishing harm and helping others.

After my recall from Italy I too was subjected to criticism and set backs. I must confess, however, that a compensation for this was provided after the war by the understanding with which I was treated by the occupation authorities, especially in the British zone.

There remains the memory of the trust I encountered in Italy from the first; it began at the Military Academy at Turin and led to many friendships. There also remains my deep respect for the vigilant and honourable conduct of Rintelen and Bismarck.

There also remains anger and indignation at those that caused or aggravated the worst accident in our history, that is, the period from 1933 to 1945. I use the word accident deliberately. For we should never succumb to the temptation of trying to fit the rise of Hitler and the Nazi period into the normal development of our history. There is no historical or socio-political inner link between the relations of Prussia or Germany to other countries at the time of Frederick the Great, Bismarck or the Imperial period and what was done to the world by the Nazi dictatorship.

The sociologist Max Weber said that those who work in the political field must have three qualities—passion, a sense of responsibility, and a sense of proportion. In those who brought about that great disaster the place of passion was taken by blind fanaticism. They lacked a sense of responsibility because they had no religious ties, no strong voice of conscience, and none of the morally-based relationship that authority should have to those

over whom authority is exercised. The place of the sense of proportion for the possible and the necessary that is so vitally important for any political success can never be taken merely by strong will and trained thinking. In the case of the Nazis it was eliminated by the intoxication of their arrogant self-confidence.

The vantage-point of Rome provided daily evidence of the correctness of Max Weber's dictum. In Italy too a sense of proportion was lacking, and politics were set on the wrong course for many years and the bow was over-stretched. But to those who tried at the last minute to quench the great self-kindled conflagration no blame should be attached. They had a hard burden to bear. To that I can testify.

Index

Abyssinia, 138
Acquarone, Pietro, Duke of, 41, 45, 48, 104, 124
Acqui Division, 144
Adam, Major Augusto, 56
Adreatine shootings, 56, 62–3
Air Force, 2, 73, 134
Air raids, 19–20, 33, 117, 121, 131
Albania, 138
Alfieri, Dino, 7, 27, 44, 110
Algeria, 12
Allies: arms production, 28, 32; Italian approaches to, 111–12, 123–32; Italian negotiations with, 114, 132–5, 142–8; signing of Armistice, 132; prisoners in Italy, 135
Alpine passes, 67–8, 117–18, 120
Alpini Division, 118
Alvisi, Alessandro, 22
Ambrosio, Colonel-General Vittorio: Klessheim meeting, 1, 8–9, 10; background, 13–14; relations with Kesselring, 13–15; impending invasion of Italy, 16; German military aid, 17, 29, 33; reports to Hitler, 27; requests to resign, 30; Feltre meeting, 33, 48; conversation with Keitel, 34; Mussolini's resignation, 45–6; German troops in Upper Italy, 67, 96, 104–5, 118; proposed arrest, 83; Operation Student, 91; proposed meeting with Germans, 94; Tarvisio meeting, 108, 110, 115–16; peace moves, 124–5, 128; negotiations with allies, 132, 135
American forces: North Africa, 12, 13; Sicily landings, 26, 28; shipping potential, 28
see also Allies

Anfuso, Filippo, 24, 64, 145, 146, 148–9
Anti-Fascist movements, 24–6
Anti-Hitler movement, 23–4, 79–81
Apennines, 126
Armistice: false rumours, 122–3; approaches made, 111–12, 123–32; negotiations, 114, 132–5, 142–8; signing, 135, 147; announcement, 135–6; German view, 149–50
Arms and equipment: supply, 2–3, 16; for Fascist Party Militia, 18–19; allied production, 28, 32; German production, 32; Italian shortage, 30, 32; Italian production, 94
Army: African campaign, 2; subordinate role to German Army, 4; supply of arms, 16, 30; discipline, 32; Piave Division, 49, 61; Brenner Pass, 67–8; support for Badoglio, 73; surrounding Rome, 85, 144; Fourth Army, 99, 118, 120; Alpini Division, 118; distribution, 118–19; Acqui Division, 144; cessation of hostilities, 144–5

Baade, General Ernst-Günther, 8, 78–9
Badoglio, Marshal Pietro: and the continuation of the war, 42, 58, 59, 66, 108, 113, 121, 125, 126–7, 149; relationship with Victor Emmanual 47; appointed head of government, 40–1, 46, 47, 48, 75, 94, 103–4; assumes office, 49–61, 67, 74–5; and communist unrest, 49, 108–9; support from Mussolini, 50–1, 70–2, 73, 148; and Mussolini's hiding place, 51, 66; and raid on German Consulate in Turin, 53; relations with von

Rintelen, 54–5; contact with Hitler, 65, 66; and the Brenner Pass, 67; proposes meeting of heads of Governments, 75, 94, 107, 126; proposed arrest, 83; and Operation Student, 89, 91; reaffirms Italy's position to von Rintelen, 91, 93–5; and German troops in Upper Italy, 108–9; and the Tarvisio meeting, 117; approaches the Allies, 121, 128–9, 132; peace moves, 123, 124–5; negotiations with the allies, 132, 136; signing of the armistice, 135–7, 147–8; surrender of Mussolini to Allies, 145–8; leaves Rome, 146

Badoglio, Mario, 102

Balkans: Italian policy towards, 7–9; withdrawal of Italian troops, 17, 118; use of Italian resources, 130, 114; possible Allied invasion of, 31, 131; news of downfall of Fascism, 57, 125; surrender of Italian troops to Germans, 144

Bastianini, Giuseppe, 5, 6, 52, 123–4

Bastico, Colonel-General Ettore, 55–6

Bedell Smith, General Walter, 134, 135

Berio, Alberto, 131, 132, 146

Berlin, Lieutenant-Colonel Hermann, 86

Bettoni, Count Sandro, 22

Bismarck, Prince Otto von: and the Klessheim meeting, 10; contact with the Italian situation, 21–3; anti-Hitler plot, 23–4; Allied arms production, 28; fears Dollmann, 64; co-operation with Badoglio government, 65; and Scorza's proposed refuge, 74; and downfall of Nazism, 77; shape of new Germany, 98–9; proposed arrest of Victor Emmanuel 108; deputises for Mackensen, 116; relieved of post, 150; conduct during war, 151

Blackshirts, 16

Boehnke, Lieutenant-Colonel Justus, 9

Bologna Meeting, 119

Bolzano, 68, 96, 104, 118

Bonivento, Renzo, 22

Bonomi, Ivanoe, 45, 46, 123, 137

Brenner frontier zone, 67–8, 117–18, 120

Brigate nere (Black Brigades), 148

Britain: declaration of war, 122; see also Allies

British forces: Sicily landings, 26, 28; air raid on Rome, 34–5; see also Allies

Buffarini-Guidi, Guido, 64

Buttlar-Brandenfels, Colonel Horst, 5, 9, 19

Calzavara 22

Campbell, Sir Ronald, 130, 131, 133

Canaris, Admiral Wilhelm, 78

Castellano, Giuseppe: Balkan question, 8; personal background, 53–4; collapse of Nazi régime, 77; use of Guariglia as scapegoat, 117; peace moves, 125, 127; approach to Allies, 128; negotiations with Allies, 132–6, 143, 146; signs armistice, 147

Cavallero, Marshal Ugo, 55

Caviglia, Marshal Enrico, 47, 48, 104

Censorship of the press, 25, 75

Cephalonia, 144

Cerutti, Vittorio, 89

Chaplains to German troops, 78–9

Chetniks, 7, 8

Chiantia, 52

China, 138

Chott, 13

Churchill, Sir Winston, 134, 145, 147

Ciano, Count Galeazzo, 89, 122, 138–9

Clausewitz, Karl von, 125

Coastal defences, 2, 3

Colle Sacro, 104

Colonna, Princess Isabella, 83, 89

Comando Supremo: Klessheim meeting, 1; arms supply, 3; Russian front, 3; Fascist Party Militia, 9; German military aid, 17, 18–19, 27, 29, 35–6; Badoglio's government, 56–7; Invasion of Sicily, 61; Ger-

man troops in Upper Italy, 66–8, 76, 82, 96, 104–5, 120; Mussolini's support, 71–2; addresses demanded, 81; von Rintelen's visit to Hitler, 91; co-operation with Germany, 101; relations with von Rintelen, 110; Tarvisio meeting, 114; withdrawal from France, 118, 119; collapse of Fascism, 125; von Rintelen's departure, 150
Communist unrest in Italy, 49, 108–9
Conforti, Gerardo, 22
Corsica, 2, 30, 119
Curfew in Rome, 41, 61
Cyrenaica, 55, 56

Dahm, Georg, 142
D'Ajeta, Marquis Blasco Lanza, 129–30, 131, 132, 146
Deakin, F. W. D., 4, 48, 124, 126, 147
De Cesare, Nicolò, 33
De Francesco, Lieutenant-Colonel Renato, 56
De Revel, Admiral Thaon, 47, 104
De Stefanis, General Giuseppe, 96
Di Raimondo, General Giovanni, 97
Djebel, 56
Doertenbach, Ulrich: Klessheim meeting, 10; contact with events in Rome, 21–3; contact with Badoglio government, 41–2, 65; change of government, 49–50; overthrow of Nazi régime, 77, 79; shape of new Germany, 98
Dollmann, Dr. Eugen: Klessheim meeting, 1, 6; relations with Hitler, 6; relations with von Mackensen, 10, 21; reports on Italian morale, 20; gives refuge to Italians, 52, and Badoglio's government, 60, 61–2, 92; restoration of Fascism, 63; sources of information, 63–4; addresses of Comando Supremo members, 81, 83; report on Guariglia, 117
Dönitz, Grand Admiral Karl, 59, 87
Dopolavoro organization, 115
Duce: see Mussolini, Vittorio

É giunta l'ora?, 25
Economic resources, 2
Eden, Sir Anthony, 124
Eisenhower, General Dwight D., 135
El Alamein, 12, 55
Elena di Savoia, Queen of Italy, 83
Equipment: see Arms and equipment

Falck, Colonel Wolfgang, 79
Farinacci, Roberto: Grand Council's last meeting, 36, 37; Mussolini's resignation, 44; seeks refuge in Germany, 51, 74; counter-measures against Badoglio, 52; contact with Dollmann, 64
Fascist Grand Council: last meeting, 36–7, 39–48, 76, 110, 139
Fascist Party: rejection by Italian officers, 16; anti-Fascist movement, 24–6; collapse, 36, 39–48, 51, 58, 72, 93, 109, 125; restoration attempts, 61, 63, 65, 70, 82–105
Fascist Party Militia, 9, 18–19, 26
Fascist Republican Government, 64, 148–9
Federzoni, Luigi, 43
Fellgiebel, General Erich, 78
Feltre meeting, 28–37, 44, 114, 115, 126
Fett, Lieutenant-Colonel Kurt, 78
Feurstein, General Valentin, 117–18
Fillipони, Major Ferdinando, 22
Food shortage, 20
France: withdrawal of Italian troops, 17, 118; Italian troops reaction to end of Fascism, 57, 125; transfer of German troops, 68, 99; Rommel in, 80; Italian Fourth Army, 99, 118, 120; Allied invasion proposed 131
Franco, General, 7
Frascati meeting, 82–6, 88, 92, 101
Freedom of speech, 25
Fummi, Luigi, 124

Galbiati, Enzo, 28, 44
Gallo, Colonel, 1
Gandin, General Antonio, 1, 144–5

Gariboldi, General Italo, 11
Gela, 26
Gericke, Herbert, 48, 71
German Army: in Sicily, 26, 27, 61,
111, 115; Hermann Göring Divi-
sion, 26; in Upper Italy, 66–8, 76,
95, 96–8, 104–5, 108–9, 114, 118,
120; Hoch- und Deutschmeister
Division, 67; Leibstandarte Adolf
Hitler, 67, 97; transfer of troops
from France, 68, 99; reaction to
Hitler's alleged death, 69–70; chap-
lains to, 78–9; 305th Division, 82;
2nd Parachute Division, 83; 3rd
Panzer Grenadier Division, 83;
Cavalry Regiment No. 3, 78;
around Rome, 96, 110, 114; 76th
Infantry Division, 97; Army Group
B, 118; occupation of Rome, 136,
144; offered as 'dowry', 143
German High Command: North
African campaign, 2, 12; Balkan
campaign, 8; contact with troops in
the field, 15; military aid to Italy,
17, 18, 27, 37; Feltre meeting, 30;
Mussolini's resignation, 37, 40;
German troops in Upper Italy, 67,
95, 96, 118, 120; and Badoglio's
appointment, 103; liberation of
Mussolini, 105; evacuates Sicily,
111; alleges the handing over of
Mussolini to the Allies, 145; and
Italy's surrender, 149–50
German military aid to Italy, 3, 7,
17–19, 26–7, 108
German Navy, 28
Girosi, Admiral Massimo, 1
Gisevius, Hans Bernd, 23–4, 77
Goebbels, Dr Josef: Italian reaction
to his speech, 4; counter measures
against Badoglio, 52; propaganda
against Italy, 120, 127; miracle
weapon, 126; on Mussolini in
Upper Italy, 149
Göring, Hermann, 6, 15, 86, 102
Government leaves Rome, 136
Grafing, 150
Gran Sasso d'Italia, 82, 146

Grand Council of Fascism, 36–7, 39–
48, 76, 110, 139
Grandi, Count Dino: dissociation
from Fascist government, 36–7;
Anti-Mussolini resolution, 42–5,
48, 103, 110; Operation Student,
89; Pact of Steel, 138
Greece, 23, 36, 144
Guariglia, Raffaele: opinion of von
Mackensen, 21; Tarvisio meeting,
66, 72, 112–17; foreign policy, 75;
proposed arrest, 83; appointment
as Foreign Minister, 104; meeting
with Mackensen, 107; approaches
to Allies, 111, 121, 128–32; continuation of the war, 112, 114;
denies capitulation, 114; used as a
scapegoat, 117; and secret weapons,
126; peace moves, 127; negotiations
with Allies, 132–3, 135

Hagen, Walter, 60, 64
Halem, General von, 90
Harbou, Joachim von, 9
Hausbrandt, Captain, 1
Hermann Göring Division, 26
Hesse, Philip, Prince of, 28
Hidaka, Ambassador Shiurokuro, 100
Himmler, Heinrich: Klessheim meeting, 9; restoration of Fascism, 63;
interviews Kappler, 91–2; Operation Student, 102
Hitler, Adolf: Klessheim meeting, 1,
5–8; and Tunisia, 2; reports from
Rintelen, 5, 100–3; revives Mussolini's spirits, 10, 34; and the Russian
front, 11, 46; and North African
campaign, 12, 13, 15; opinion of
Kesselring, 13; lack of visits to
Mediterranean area, 15; Italy's
military collapse, 17–18; assassi-
nation plots, 23–4; plans for overthrow of, 25, 77, 79–80; and Sicily
invasion, 26–7, 111; military aid for
Italy, 27; Feltre conference, 28–34;
reaction to Badoglio's government,
49; final downfall, 51; abduction of
Mussolini, 51, 70; Mussolini's

resignation, 60, 65, 70–2; counter measure to Badoglio's government, 52, 60–1, 82; and Fascist Republican Government, 64, 148–9; and Mussolini's hiding place, 66; alleged death, 69–70; and Colonel Baade, 78; Operation Student, 86, 87, 88, 90–1, 100–2; greetings from Kesselring, 96; fears arrest in Italy, 107; Tarvisio meeting, 111, 116; Balkan front, 114; Bologna meeting, 119; ignores Italy's predicament, 121; wanted the war, 122; and Italian peace moves, 124, 127; secret weapons, 126; abandonment of Italy, 127; prepares to break with Italy, 128; Pact of Steel, 138–9; shooting of Italian officers, 144; and Italian attachés in Berlin, 150

Hitler Youth, 81

Hoare, Sir Samuel, 133

Hoch- und Deutschmeister Division, 67

Hofer, Franz, 118

Honour, 125

Invasion of France, 131

Invasion of Italy, 2, 3, 16, 17, 18, 19, 30, 67, 97, 98, 99, 108, 121, 144

Invasion of Sicily, 13, 26–8, 34, 57, 61, 70, 73

Italy, see North Italy and Upper Italy

Jandl, Lieutenant-Colonel Johann, 68–9

Januzzi, Lieutenant-Colonel, 1

Japan, 138

Japanese Ambassador, 39, 42

Jeschek, Hans-Heinrich, 141–2

Jews, 5, 49

Jodl, General Alfred: lack of visits to the front, 15; communications cut, 40; Operation Student, 87; Bologna meeting, 119–21; and the Italian armistice, 137

Junge, Captain Wolf, 82, 86

Kaltenbrunner, Otto, 117

Kappler, Herbert, 60, 62, 91–2

Keitel, Wilhelm: Klessheim meeting, 8; lack of visits to Mediterranean area, 15; Feltre meeting, 34; communications cut, 40; and Badoglio's government, 66; and von Rintelen's visits to Hitler, 91; proposed meeting with Ambrosio, 94; Operation Student, 100; Tarvisio meeting, 108, 111–12; von Rintelen's replacement, 150

Kennan, George, 134

Kessel, Albrecht von, 98

Kesselring, Field-Marshal Albert: North African campaign, 13; relations with Ambrosio, 13–15; confidence of the Italians, 15; and Sicily, 26, 111; Mussolini's resignation, 39, 40; change of government, 49–50; asylum to Italians, 52; and Badoglio's government, 58–9; Mussolini's birthday, 66, 71; Operation Student, 82–7, 91, 92, 101; greetings to Hitler, 96; German troops in Italy, 96–8; occupation of Rome, 136; German troops offered as 'dowry', 143

Klessheim meeting, 1–11, 83, 144

Kürenberg, Joachim von, 62–3

La Maddalena Island, 146

Langen, Kirk von, 53

Lavoro Fascista, 103

Leibstandarte Adolf Hitler, 67, 97

Leopold III, King of the Belgians, 93, 123

Libya, 4, 55, 138

Löwisch, Admiral Werner, 59

Luftwaffe, 17, 27, 79, 143

Mackensen, Hans-Georg von: Klessheim meeting, 1; official reports, 10, 23; Italian morale, 20–1; and Sicily landings, 28; Mussolini's resignation, 36, 41; reports on change of government, 49–50; sends Farinacci to Germany, 51; offers asylum to Italians, 51, 52–3; and raids on German consulate in

Turin, 53; and Badoglio's government, 58, 62, 65, 75–6, 95; Mussolini's birthday, 66; offers Scorza refuge in Germany, 74, 76; and addresses of Comando Supremo, 86; Operation Student, 89–90; Italian Japanese relationship, 100; and possible arrest of Crown Prince, 107; collapse of Fascism, 109; return to Germany, 116; Pact of Steel, 139

Maglione, Luigi, 123, 124, 129

Malta, 13, 147

Maltzahn, Colonel Günther von, 79

Marchesi, Major Luigi: last meeting of the Grand Council, 39–40; and rejoicings in Rome, 41; and Badoglio's government, 56–7; collapse of Nazi régime, 77; German attitude towards Italy, 109–11; signing of the armistice, 135; announcement of the armistice, 136

Mareth, 13

Maria, 25–6, 40, 77

Maria-José di Savoia, Crown Princess, 83, 123

Marras, General Efisio Luigi, 66, 94, 118, 150

Melchiori, Alessandro, 10–11, 34, 55

Mellano, Colonel Pietro, 8

Merchant shipping, 2

Mihailovich, Draža, 7

Milan: air raids, 131

Military aid to Italy, 3, 7, 17–19, 26–7, 30–2, 108, 115

Militia, 9, 18–19, 26

Mollier, Hans Heinrich, 39

Monterotondo, 96, 98

Montezemolo, Colonel Giuseppe Cordero Lanza di: Klessheim meeting, 1, 8, 9; arms for Fascist Party Militia, 18–19; Mussolini and the Rome air raid, 33; at the Ministry of Interior, 54–5; personal background, 56; and Hitler's attitude to Mussolini's resignation, 71, 72; and Badoglio's government, 72–6, 95, 96; continuation of the war, 125

Morale, 4, 20–1, 35–6, 117

Morgantini, Major Manlio, 56, 73

Mussolini, Benito: health, 1, 4, 9, 10, 26, 42, 66; Klessheim meeting, 1, 5–7, 9, 11; and Russian front, 3; Fascist Republic Militia, 9, 19; confidants of, 10–11; and African campaign, 10–11, 55–6; giving way to Hitler, 14, 126; and German military aid, 17, 27, 33–4; loyalty to German alliance, 20; von Mackensen reports on, 20, 58; invasion of Sicily, 26–7; Feltre meeting, 28–34; effect of air raid on Rome, 33, 34; disillusioned with Hitler, 34; arrest, 46, 48; attitude to new government, 50–1; in hiding, 51, 66, 70, 146; birthday present, 66; Fascist Republican Government, 69, 148–9; release by Hitler, 70, 82, 104; support to Badoglio, 50–1, 70–2, 73, 148; and the Balkans, 113–14; attempts to prevent war, 122; retires Badoglio, 123; peace moves, 123, 124, 127; Italy not ready for war, 138; Pact of Steel, 139; possibility of being surrendered to the Allies, 145–8

Mussolini, Vittorio, 51

Navy, 2, 31, 73, 134

Nazi régime: overthrow, 77, 79–80; German criticism, 80–1

Negotiations with the Allies: prospects of, 111; false rumours of, 122–3; approaches made, 123–32; negotiations, 132–5; signing of armistice, 135

Neubauer, Captain Karl-Heinz, 82

Newspapers, censorship, 75

North African campaign, 2, 4, 9, 12–19, 23, 30, 36, 44, 55, 149

North Italy: invasion possibility, 18, 67, 97, 98, 99, 108; communist unrest, 49, 108–9; German troops, 76, 95, 96–8, 104–5, 108–9, 114, 118, 120; Fascist Republican Government, 148–9

Nurra, Colonel, 54, 56–7

Oil shortages, 2
Operation Student, 81–105, 128, 137, 151
Osborne, Sir D'Arcy, 129
Oshima, Hiroshi, 100

Pact of Steel, 137–42
Palazzo Venezia, 36, 39
Papen, Franz von, 112
Parma, 149
Pavolini, Alessandro, 52–3
Pansa, Mario, 108
Peraldo, Lieutenant-Colonel, 8
Philip of Hesse, Prince, 28
Piave Division, 49, 61
Piazza di Spagna, Rome, 40–1
Pietromarchi, Count Luca, 8, 10
Pirelli, Alberto, 131, 132
Poland, 132, 139
Poli, Sandri, 25
Political trials, 149
Post Office, 73
Press censorship, 25, 75
Preziosi, Giovanni, 51
Puntoni, General Paolo, 47, 93, 128, 132–3, 136

Quirinal, 40, 93, 128

Railways, 73, 96, 97
Raw materials, 2, 32
Ribbentrop, Joachim von: Klessheim meeting, 5, 6, 8–9; and the Balkan question, 8–9; military aid to Italy, 27; counter measures against Badoglio, 51–2, 60, 74; Tarvisio meeting, 66, 72, 111–17, 130, 131, 141; and Scorza's capitulation, 76; proposed German Italian meeting, 107; Britain's entry into the war, 122; Germany not ready for war, 138–9
Riccardi, Admiral Arturo, 59
Rintelen, General Enno von: Klessheim meeting, 1; reports on situation in Italy, 3–4; dinner party, 15; reports on impending invasion, 16; and arms deliveries, 19; position in Roman society, 22; report on

Italian reaction to Feltre meeting, 35–6; reprimanded, 36; report on Grand Council meeting, 37; and Mussolini's resignation, 39, 40; and Badoglio's appointment, 47; state of siege declared in Rome, 49; and Badoglio's government, 49–50, 58, 65, 75–6; relations with Badoglio, 54–5; car accident, 55; invasion of Sicily, 61; restoration of Fascism, 63; and German troops in Upper Italy, 67, 76, 108–9; Mussolini–Badoglio's relationship, 70–1; overthrow of Nazi régime, 77; addresses of Comando Supremo, 81–2; Operation Student, 87, 88, 90–104; possible arrest of Victor Emmanuel, 107; Tarvisio meeting, 109–11; relationship with Comando Supremo, 110; Bologna meeting, 119–21; relieved of post, 150–1
Roatta, General Mario: impending invasion of Italy, 16; German military aid, 17; German troops in Upper Italy, 67, 97–8; Sicily, 115; Bologna meeting, 119–21
Rocco, Minister, 74–5
Roman Catholic Church, 5; see also Vatican
Rome: air raids on, 33, 34–5, 94, 117; curfew, 41, 61; Italian troops around, 85, 144; German troops around, 96, 110, 114; declared open city, 117, 121; proposals for occupation by Allied troops, 135; German occupation, 136, 144
Rommel, Field-Marshal Erwin: African campaign, 10, 44, 55; Brenner frontier zone, 67–8; Upper Italy, 68, 118; overthrow of Nazi régime, 79–80; Bologna meeting, 119, 120; abandonment of Italy, 126
Roosevelt, President Franklin D., 134
Rossi, General Francesco: demonstrations in Rome, 41; state of siege declared in Rome, 49; German troop movement in Italy, 61; possible arrest, 85; meeting with

Westphal,99;Tarvisio meeting, 110;
Bologna meeting, 119
Ruge, Admiral Friedrich, 59
Rumanian oil, 31, 126
Rundstedt, Field-Marshal Gert von,
57
Russia: need for German troops in, 3,
27; armistice with, 6, 11, 46;
German policy towards, 14; use
of Italian troops against, 30;
and prevention of another front
in Europe, 31; transfer of troops
from, 67, 68; German Embassy in,
150

Salò Republic, 64, 148-9
Sardinia, 2, 17, 30, 135, 138, 146
Schmidt, Paul-Otto, 32
Schuchardt, Colonel Karl, 91
Scorza, Carlo: and German military
aid, 27; last meeting of the Grand
Council, 44; offered refuge in Ger-
many, 52, 74; and Badoglio's
government, 73, 75-6
Scuero, Antonio, 123
Senger und Etterlin, General Frido
von, 78, 80, 149
Serbian nationalists, 7, 8
Sicily: coastal defences, 2; invasion,
13, 26-8, 34, 57, 61, 70, 73; rein-
forcements for, 17; loss to allies,
30-1, 125; German troops in, 78,
86, 115, 121; German evacuation,
111; Italian troops, 118; signing of
the armistice, 135, 147
Signing of armistice, 135, 147
Skorzeny, Otto, 82, 92, 146
Spain, 7
Speidel, Hans, Lieutenant-General,
80
SS, 9, 63, 112, 119
Stalingrad, 3, 61
Stauffenberg, Count Claus Schenk
von, 78
Steengracht von Moyland, Gustav
Adolf, 7, 28, 100
Straits of Messina, 61, 79
Strohm, Gustav, 68

Strong, General Kenneth William,
134
Student, General Kurt, 82-6; see also
Operation Student
Supply lines: Sicily landings, 28
Suvich, Fulvio, 89
Swiss Foreign Ministry, 131

Tarvisio meeting, 66, 101, 108-18,
131, 132, 141
Tedder, Air Marshal Arthur William,
35
Testa, Temistocle, 74
Theodoli, Don Livio, 8
Transport system, 67, 73, 96, 97
Tripoli, 10-11
Tunis, 5, 9
Tunisia, 2, 12-19, 20
Turin: attack on German consulate,
53, 113; Military Academy, 151

U-boats, 32
Umberto di Savoia, Crown-Prince:
proposed arrest, 83, 107, 108;
proposed meeting with German
leaders, 115-16; negotiations with
the allies, 123, 132
Upper Italy: invasion possibility, 18,
67, 97, 98, 99, 108; Communist
unrest, 49, 108-9; German troops,
76, 95, 96-8, 104-5, 108-9, 114,
118, 120; Fascist Republican Government, 148-9

Vailati, Vanna, 128
Vatican: and Operation Student, 85,
88, 92, 93; Rome declared an
open city, 117; and continuation of
the war, 121; peace feelers through,
122-4, 129
Veltheim, Colonel Herbert von,
108
Verdross, Alfred von, 142
Verona, 149
Villa Savoia, 40, 48, 84, 85, 92, 93
Vitetti, Count Leonardo, 10, 83
Victor Emmanuel III, King of Italy:
and Mussolini's resignation, 39-46;

appoints Badoglio Prime Minister,
46–8, 75, 103, 104; and the fall of
Fascism, 49, 151; and continuation
of the war, 113, 127; proposed
meetings with Hitler, 66, 107, 115,
126; and Mussolini's loyalty, 70, 71,
149; and Operation Student, 83,
84, 87, 88, 93; approaches to the
Allies, 102, 108, 111, 121, 124, 128,
129; rebukes Crown Princess, 123;
negotiations with Allies, 132, 135;
leaves Rome, 136
Volpi, 89

Warlimont, General Walter, 78, 95,
143
Washington, 123
Weapons: see Arms and equipment
Weber, Max, 151–2
Weise, Colonel General Hubert, 79,
80
Weizsäcker, Ernst, 93, 121
Wenner, Max, 19, 81
Westphal, Major-General Siegfried,
82–7, 99, 101, 136

Zeitzler, General Kurt, 91

DATE DUE